Dedication

Dedicated to the memory of Kathleen,
a stranger whose dying I witnessed in hospital.

In your hours of semi-consciousness
struggling painfully throughout the night of your dying
you taught me so much in such a short space of time –
about the preciousness of human life, courage
and the will to live against impossible odds.

Death took you in the end but you gave brave battle.
I would have been proud to have known you in life
and I will never forget you. Rest in peace.

'If we wish to die well, we must learn how to live well'
The Dalai Lama

Emerald Guides
Brighton BN2 4EG

ISBN 184716 038 7
ISBN 13: 9781847160386

Printed by
Biddles Limited Kings Lynn Norfolk
Cover design by Bookworks Islington

CONTENTS

HISTORIC & COMMUNITY CONTEXT

QUALITY: EVIDENCE & DIAGNOSIS

DIAGRAMS

KEY LEARNING

INTRODUCTION

Welcome to my book, which is the 2nd of a two part series on mental health within communities.

In this book we explore the journey of patient care; from first signs of illness, through diagnosis, treatment and aftercare. I've covered a broad range of topics to give you plenty of material on which to base your future studies; exploring areas that fire your imagination and passion.

If you are new to the field or a patient, friend or carer and reading for basic information about mental illness do not worry about jargon because I write in narrative style and include comprehensive glossaries. My aim is to clarify not to baffle!

During the writing of these two books, I underwent a great deal of suffering but in time, experiences will add my perception about living and working in communities, which is not an easy task for anyone. Professionals are sometimes cagey about sharing their life experiences, but for me this is a way of becoming your own learning tool and sharing that learning with others.

I have been dogged all my life by depression and a mild form of autism. The depression manifests as my personal stress gauge so it has become a useful tool when it manifests. The autism means that I resist social occasions; but that enables me to research and hone my writing skills These conditions have a positive advantage in mental health because they add richness and texture, as well as giving me a many faceted viewpoint; patient, mental health worker, citizen; to say nothing of my work in private healthcare.

I hold several views on the NHS. I am not a supporter generally, because it has become an unwieldy crushing machine, with the sort of tiny budgets that breed negative characteristics within staff groups, however, I do support the idea of affordable patient care and affordable career training for staff.

There is a traditional conflict between NHS and private practice – NHS practitioners and have ready-made lists of patients; private therapists have to advertise and pay overheads. However, there is a middle way.

I believe the paper by Susan Dr Parenti for a new future for the United States NHS merits further reading. Years ago, I had a vision of a new healthcare system replacing the cumbersome NHS, based on local services. This is what Dr Parenti is now advocating; an integrated system, locally based. An updated version of the paper will be available soon, on the Patch Adams website.

I hope you will enjoy one of my latest innovations. Humour has a place in mental health as you will come to see when you read about Patch Adams. Ann Collins is an unsung yet talented craftswoman who works with parchment. I asked if she would re-interpret my simple diagrams and she has done so with a deft, humorous yet sensitive touch. I hope she decides to continue as a book illustrator and am delighted to launch a potentially rewarding new career.

Although I share the stated values of the publisher whole-heartedly remember these books contain my personal views and I alone am responsible for them.

Accessibility is the aim of this publisher and myself as author. Jargon and mystique are demeaning to writer and reader alike for it sets them apart. How can we learn from such distances? Please let me know if I ever stray from the path of clarity!

I cannot tell you what to do in your daily work as a mental health worker, for you will find your own way through daily practice. All I can give is my experience and knowledge, from the point of view of a therapist and sometime patient.

If you have ideas or suggestions for future editions I welcome them. If you find errors, write and tell me but please find the remedy first. You see, my heart is as vulnerable as yours.

Thanks to the many organisations who assisted me and a small thumbs down to the one organisation [or should I say person] who was not.

I hope you enjoy this book and that it will answer some of your many questions. Use it as a starting point for your own journey into the fascinating, often tragic but also triumphant world of mental illness.

Marianne Richards
31st May 2007

The Bridge

Sitting by your side
I try to find the words.
They will not come.

Your wounded soul is torn with grief
That cannot find relief.

I catch your eye
You catch mine.
I hold out my hand.
You take it.
A bridge is forged.

I hold your hand
As the sky is falling
The sky is falling.

I will hold your hand
Though the sky is falling
The sky is falling.

Marianne C Richards
August 1992

Acknowledgements

I would like to thank the following

- National Institute for Health & Clinical Excellence
- The British Film Institute
- i-stock photo community
- All my reviewers for giving up their precious free time
- University of Bath
- Mark and the gardening team of B&Q Longwell Green, for welcoming me to their world

A Short History of Medicine [from The Quote Garden]
2000 B.C. - "Here, eat this root."
1000 B.C. - "That root is heathen, say this prayer."
1850 A.D. - "That prayer is superstition, drink this potion."
1940 A.D. - "That potion is snake oil, swallow this pill."
1985 A.D. - "That pill is ineffective, take this antibiotic."
2000 A.D. - "That antibiotic is artificial. Here, eat this root."
http://www.quotegarden.com/medical.html

1 Overview – History of Mental Illness

Contents of this Chapter:

The above epigram is longer than the others in this book but it is so apt I wanted you to share it with me. It is the epitome of the changing fashion in medical treatment which spirals over the centuries to arrive at the starting point again - with new insights. For me, that sums up this field.

Patients are now eschewing medicine in favour of traditional treatments, many taken from the ancient civilisations in the East. In a world which is daily rocked with change it seems we are reaching for old home comforts.

This book, second in the series, is about diagnosis and treatment. As in **Understanding Mental Illness**, I will offer vignettes to illuminate the facts. These are not real people but an amalgamation of characteristics which represent symptoms of mental health problems.

I will start with an overview of Part 1, which gave a brief history of mental illness and a description of how it fits in a community setting. I feel it important to repeat, that you cannot understand the treatment of mental illness, without an understanding of the social and historic context of its setting.

Prehistoric Mental Illness

Mental illnesses have not always been recognised as medical conditions. Early evidence shows prehistoric men considered afflictions of the mind to be brought about by evil spirits. They did not have our awareness of the human psyche [mind].

Remedies were variously: being cast out by the community, reparation through sacrifice [animal or human] or having these spirits or demons cast out by priests or shamans [holy men]. Sometimes demons were cast out by trepanning, the practice of drilling through the skull to the brain. Thus, early man invented a type of psychosurgery, not knowing the practice would still be carried out thousands of years later, albeit for different reasons.

The Romans

Some ancient Romans believed madness was caused through family curses which had to be laid to rest through the actions of a hero who was challenged to slay a beast or even a human relative. Similar stories occur in many mythological stories:

Beast slayers; George and the Dragon, Theseus and the Minotaur, Perseus and Medusa

Family slayers: Iphigenia and Agamemnon, followed in the same family by Orestes and Clytemnestra [one of the earliest family revenge killings!]

Hippocrates, a Greek Doctor and Philosopher, overturned the conventional view of madness as punishment by gods. He described three types of mental disorder:

- brain fever
- mania
- melancholia

Hippocrates and Galen, around the same period in history, studied the four vital body fluids [which they called humours] which were believed to give man his vitality. When these humours became unbalanced they were thought to cause illnesses of the body and mind.

I talked about how this system is closely allied with the holistic beliefs of Chinese and Western alternative medicines.

In book one, there is a diagram of the four humours which I have paralleled with:

- the 4 elements in alchemy [earth, air, fire, water]
- the 4 seasons [spring, summer, autumn, winter]

In recognising the relationship between these systems you can see their archetypal overtones; that is, how different cultures hold parallel views.

Remember, until recently the disciplines of religion, science and medicine were once part of one overarching religious system ruled over by powerful people – the priests or shamans. The shamans were the priest/healers of their time and it was their knowledge which held the key to their power.

Key Learning 1 The Gods and Madness
Early medicine was based around religion. Mental illnesses were believed to be inflicted by angry gods or evil spirits.

The holistic system originated in the East in ancient times but is now a world wide cultural phenomena. Holism is about healing the body, mind and spirit, rather than seeing illness as an effect of one of these. In the West, the tide is turning towards a more holistic view as conventional medicine falls from favour and patients increasingly turn to spirituality and alternative medicine – particularly in the case of mental illness.

The Romans were familiar with depressive illness and treated it humanely with warm baths, music and well-lit rooms as in the Temples of Light. Such treatments would still be recognised as beneficial. Even the curious Roman treatment of putting patients in a bath with electric eels has parallels with electric shock therapy.

Plato's system of locking up madmen within their own home, rather than state funded buildings, was common up until the 19th century, when our Victorian forbears started the practice of locking the insane in large Asylums in the countryside.

Medieval Beliefs

There was a mix of beliefs in medieval times. Insanity [emotional or behavioural problems] was considered divine retribution or the result of witchcraft, but by the 17th century a more enlightened attitude existed, as in the case of Emma de Beston.

Emma de Beston received fair treatment at the hands of the local church inquisition as she suffered various episodes of madness. Inquisitions were local church appointed courts, not all on the lines of the Spanish Inquisition of the Catholic Church.

Bethlehem Asylum (Bethlam or Bedlam) was set up through public subscription in 1377 to lock up the insane. Early Asylums contained a mix of mental patients, who might have what we now know as separate elements:

- major mental illness
- forensic [criminal] mental illness
- organic disease
- brain injury

There was no distinction between these at this time in history as little was known about the function of the physical brain or ephemeral mind.

The term bedlam was coined to describe the chaos and noise associated with patients of Bethlam. These poor wretches had no proper treatment apart from the cruel practices I described in book 1, which must have added to their distress and confusion. Screaming, banging and shouting continued to be common features on psychiatric wards, before medication calmed patients' psychotic symptoms.

Key Learning 2 Witchcraft & Madness
By the Middle Ages, strange behaviours were likely to be put down to witchcraft and the instigator hung or burnt as a witch.

The Sixteenth Century

By the 16th Century, mental illness became recognised as such rather than visitations by evil spirits. Interestingly, this belief came at the same time as churches losing their power to secular rulers. Witchcraft had been very profitable for the business of religious leaders.

I described how Lazar [leper] houses became disused as leprosy started to die out [the more positive result of the isolation of lepers from the community]. These large buildings were re-used as Asylums to house the insane.

However, wanderers, beggars and prostitutes also found themselves in early Asylums because mental illness also included anyone considered a social misfit. Much as the patients sent to sea in the ships of fools [described in Michael Foucault's book], this incarceration was thought to be for their own good.

By Victorian times Asylums might house upwards of 1000 patients on large, open wards with no privacy. Clothing came from the hospital linen store cupboard and was communal. Food was supplemented with vegetables grown in the large kitchen gardens.

There would have been very few visitors, because being 'sent to the asylum' was considered on the same social level as a visit to a brothel, probably more so.

Key Learning 3 Separation from Community
By the 16th century, the age of travel and exploration, insane people are housed outside the community or sent to sea for 'cure'.

Lobotomy

I have already mentioned trepanning carried out by ancient Neolithic civilisations. A modern type of psychosurgery is lobotomy, first carried out by Egas Moniz in 1935 but now very rarely used and certainly not in the mode of Moniz [with an ice pick].

Go and see the movie 'One Flew Over The Cuckoos Nest' for a graphic depiction of the effects of lobotomy. Its ending is very Hollywood but it is a valuable experience for the mental health student. Watch out for evil Nurse Ratched; a realistic portrayal!

Moniz won the 1949 Nobel Prize for his work but by 1975 this brutal practice ceased as it had been discovered to be ineffective. Many thousands of patients had had their futures destroyed by this barbaric operation, which is not reversible. In a twist of fate, Moniz was murdered by a patient he had lobotomised.

Charcot [1835 - 1893] & Breuer [1842 - 1925]

Jean Martin Charcot was the first modern therapist to use a talking cure. People often credit Freud with this distinction probably because the term was first used by one of Freud's patients to describe how she was cured of her neurosis. Never forget your debt, dear reader, to hypnosis and hypnotherapy!

Charcot and his colleague Joseph Breuer used hypnosis to cure patients with hysterical paralyses [now called conversion disorders]. Freud collaborated with both men early in his career. Breuer and Freud named the hypnotic effect catharsis or cathexis after the Greek word for cleansing or discharging.

Sigmund Freud

Under hypnosis, Freud's patients talked about their problems and when they awoke found themselves cured of neuroses. Freud eventually abandoned hypnosis because he came to believe the therapeutic relationship [relationship between therapist and patient] was the crux of cure and not the hypnotic state or the process of cathexis.

Freud developed psychoanalysis [psyche is Greek for mind] which is the process by which he analysed patients symbolic dreams. His life work was in attempting to understand the subconscious mind, a process continued by his pupil Jung.

Carl Jung - Analytical Psychology

Carl Jung was a follower of Freud but eventually split with him to found analytical psychology. Jung's work was based on understanding the personality. Jung coined the terms introvert and extrovert to describe two major aspects of personality:

- introvert - inner reflective
- extrovert - worldly and sociable

Jung was deeply interested in philosophy, world mythology and religion. He noted the similarity between the myths of different cultures despite the fact there were no direct links between the cultures which spawned them.

Common types in myths were the hero, wise man and fool. In the hero myth, a man is born of a virgin is sacrificed and through his resurrection he redeems his people. The hero myth has commonality though many religious cultures. Jung realized there must be unconscious links between people down generations and across cultures, as he could not otherwise account for these similarities.

If you want to read more about myths I recommend:

- Carl Jung; Man and his Symbols
- Joseph Campbell; The Hero with a Thousand Faces
- The Larousse Book of World Mythology
- Standard Stories from the Opera [many operas are based on myths]

Key Learning 4 The Rise of Analysis
With the mentally ill incarcerated in large numbers, doctors of the day had plenty of material to conduct research into illnesses of the mind.

Jung proposed, after years of study, that we all have archetypical characters or sub-personalities. That is not to say separate characters, but that a different archetype will come forward in different situations. Jung called his two main archetypes his no 1 and no 2 personality. I have seen my own wise old man in a very vivid dream. It is an interesting exercise to try to find your own major archetypes, by studying your dreams and by reverie or imagination.

Through studying patients Jung concluded that neurosis is a failure to integrate archetypes into the personality. The work of a Jungian Analyst is to assist patients towards integration and maturation of the personality; a process Jung termed individuation.

Jung's work on archetypes lead to his theory of the collective unconscious - the carrier which allows tribal memories to be individually retained across generations. The term unconscious refers to the fact that we are not aware of archetypal memories except under certain conditions:

- The symbolism of dreams
- de ja vue – an instinct of having been somewhere, when logically you know you haven't
- during reverie or reflective moments - memories jump into consciousness
- memories unconnected with our life but which appear to recall past events [some therapists believe these are living memories of past lives]

Behavioural Therapies

I described in the first book of this series the experiments on behaviourism by Watson, Skinner and Pavlov who showed how animal behaviour can be modified through training.

You may have heard of Pavlov's experiments where dogs were taught to salivate on the ring of a bell (before their food appeared) by being conditioned to do so.

A bell was rung before the dog's food was presented to them, and thereafter they salivated when the bell was rung. A bit like a man buying a sports car after seeing a nubile girl in the advertisement for it; he is already salivating before his credit card is out of his pocket – the pity of it is, he doesn't even get the reward.

Key Learning 5 The Behaviourists

A group of Psychologists believed maladaptive human behaviour could be treated through training behaviour or thinking.

This new field of psychology added an educational view of human emotional actions, based on recognising patterns of human behaviour which they called cognitive [cognition = recognise] therapy.

By recognising, challenging and changing faulty thinking patterns, the negative emotions associated with them and the resulting behaviours could be changed.

This is not rocket science if you think about it – how does a child learn to speak? By imitating its parents. And to behave? Through watching and copying its parents.

Behavioural and cognitive therapy were combined into cognitive-behavioural therapy which is popular due to its ratification by NICE. It is now losing ground to brief therapy in Primary Care being more time consuming and more expensive.

[Note; a cheaper option is self help, also ratified by NICE. I am sure this will be converted into an official 'therapy' with training organisations, umbrellas etc!]

Key Learning 6 The Cognitive Triangle

A hypothetical link between thinking, feeling and behaviour; changing thinking or behaviour affects resulting feeling. See diagram.

Brief Therapy - Milton Erickson

In the 1970's Erickson (an American Psychiatrist) pioneered a quirky method which had patients flocking to his clinics.

Erickson was a communicator fascinated with the symbolic use of language. He learned to deeply understand his patients, through studying what he called the patient's map of the world; how they communicated through metaphors [symbolic language].

Through Erickson's natural empathy, patients trusted him with their deepest secrets. Erickson came to believe that everyone has the key to resolving their own problems and it is the work of the therapist is to help them re-discover these strategies and apply them to current problems. This was the basis on which he built his restorative therapy – teaching them what they had forgotten, as he might say.

Erickson advocated auto-hypnosis whereby the patient, in a relaxed or trance state, could imagine themselves free of their problem. From that starting point, Erickson encouraged patients to complete tasks which would enhance the healing effect.

Key Learning 7 Brief Therapy

Brief therapies based on re-training, using the unconscious mind to bypass the resistance of the conscious.

Anti Psychiatric Movement - 60's and 70's:

Psychiatrists Szaz and Laing held the view that mental illness did not exist but was a construct of society. Laing considered the symptoms of madness to be symbolic insights, in much the same way as dreams. The anti-psychiatric movement grew as service users, frustrated with side effects of drugs and no effective drug therapies sought other answers to their suffering.

The anti-psychiatry books by Szaz, Laing and their followers make interesting reading especially with the growing preference of 21st century patients towards complementary and eco therapies.

Key Learning 8 Return of Anti Psychiatry
The anti psychiatry movement of Szaz and Laing is starting to return, with growing mistrust of medicine.

Virtual Brains - computer simulation

The last part of my brief tour of the history of mental illness covered the astonishing rate at which computer-simulated (virtual) human brains are being built.

This will stimulate faster research results particularly where there are complex factors such as faulty genes. There have been incredible breakthroughs on such diverse topics as cancer and schizophrenia enabling scientists to understand and find treatments for these devastating diseases.

****

Figure 1 A Victorian Asylum

Four views of St John's Asylum, Stone.

The building has now been demolished, making way for a modern housing estate.

Summary of Key Learning Points:

Key Learning 1 The Gods and Madness
Early beliefs were based around religion. Mental illnesses were believed to be inflicted by angry gods or evil spirits.

Key Learning 2 Witchcraft & Madness
By the Middle Ages, strange behaviours were likely to be put down to witchcraft, and the instigator hung or burnt as a witch.

Key Learning 3 Separation from Community
By the 16th century, the age of travel and exploration, insane people housed outside the community or sent to sea for 'cure'.

Key Learning 4 The Rise of Analysis
With the mentally ill incarcerated in large numbers, doctors had plenty of material to conduct research into illnesses of the mind.

Key Learning 5 The Behaviourists
A group of Psychologists believed maladaptive human behaviour could be treated through re-training behaviour or thinking.

Key Learning 6 The Cognitive Triangle
Hypothetical links between thinking, feeling and behaviour; by changing thinking or behaviour the resulting feeling can be altered. See diagram.

Key Learning 7 Brief Therapy
Brief therapies based on re-training, using the unconscious mind to bypass the resistance of the conscious.

Key Learning 8 Return of Anti Psychiatry
The anti psychiatry movement of Szaz and Laing is starting to return, with growing mistrust of medicine.

'words don't just reflect reality, they create reality'
Jose Silva, Silva Mind Control

2 Language

Contents of this Chapter:
Hutu and Tutsi tribes
Jews, Gypsies, Disabled and Mentally Ill
Scapegoating Communities

In the first of this series, I talked about language and how this affects how we see people. Some historic language now causes offence although at the time the meanings were not generally meant as pejorative:

- mad
- lunatic
- crippled

Language is often used in jocular fashion, such as young people calling their mates psycho or crazy. But language can have a more serious effects; it can stigmatise and leave people open to isolation and bullying. Perhaps it is pertinent to ask such people if they would like being called 'dum-dum' or idiot – or perhaps they would see it as a badge of honour rather than cause for shame.

Historically, name calling has been used by unscrupulous people – from gangs to totalitarian states - at an early stage in the process of isolating or scapegoating individuals, groups or whole nations, prior to wiping them out. Individual, corporate or national bullies commonly use language to bait or goad, particularly if they are supported in communities where compassion is rare. One only has to think of examples from recent history:

1 Hutu and Tutsi tribes

The Hutu and Tutsi tribes were traditional enemies of long standing. The Hutu's at one time had been an underclass and cultivated a desire for revenge.

In 1994, there was a massacre of the Tutsis in which nearly half a million people were murdered using foreign-imported machetes. This massacre had clearly been well organised.

Historic traditions worked against the moderate Tutsi's, who were scape-goated by extremist Hutu's. The country will take many decades to recover and there are millions of refugees still to fearful to return to their country of birth.

2 Jews, Gypsies, Disabled and Mentally Ill

Lead by Hitler, German Nazis subjected Jews, Gypsies, disabled and mentally ill people to pograms; they were murdered in their millions through starvation, the gas chamber and assassination by SS troups.

Ordinary German working people had been convinced that these were racially impure people who had degenerated the pure Aryan gene pool. These outcast people were also blamed for Germany's lack of status in the world.

3 Scapegoating Communities

On a smaller scale, individuals or communities who lack confidence, education or a sense of purpose tend to isolate individuals who appear to threaten them by virtue of having something they don't; goods, money, intellect, position or power. This process is called scapegoating. Bullying and scapegoating are no more than small-scale warfare.

Unscrupulous leaders of bad communities find it relatively easy to glorify themselves by appearing to rid the community of a perceived threat; through murder, loss of dignity, ridicule or undermining.

Unenlightened bigots are dangerous and a lost cause; you have only to think about the recent bombings. These people enjoy havoc because it makes them feel important – no matter what the cost to others. And, naturally, they are exploited by leaders with power agendas of their own – they are merely lambs to the slaughter if they had the intellect to see it.

The difference between thinking and dum-dum communities is that the former will eventually be ashamed of their actions; the latter will laugh raucously and continue as before. These are interesting factors which I will discuss in a future book on individual and corporate bullying.

Key Learning 9 Language of Stigma

Language is a double-edged sword and can be used to separate and isolate, as well as identify truths or conditions.

****

Figure 2 Potential Causal Factors for Mental Illness

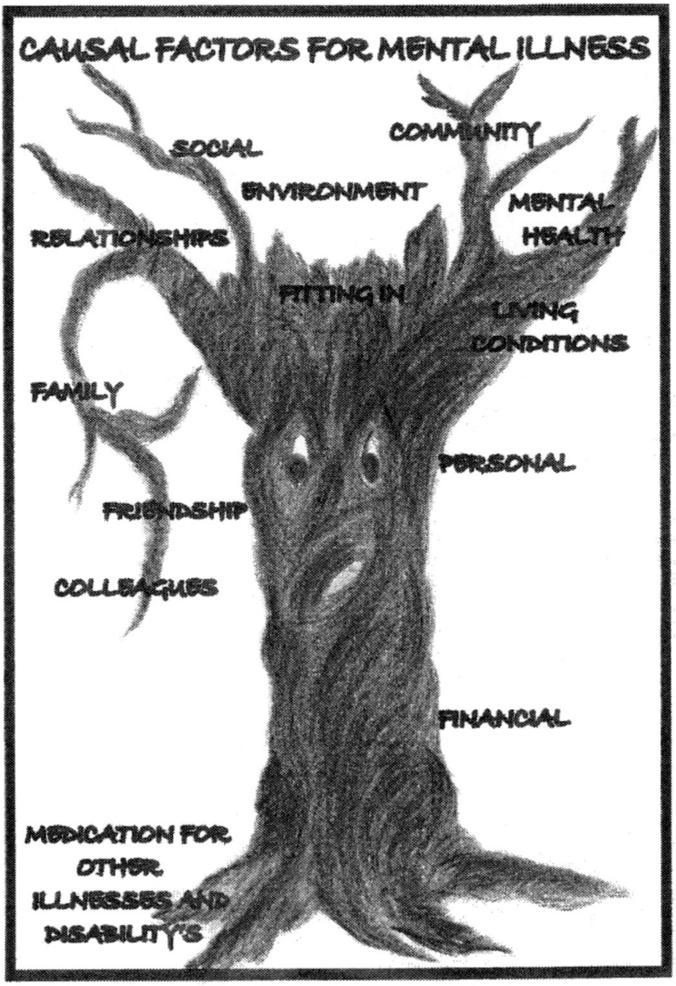

'To think otherwise than our contemporaries think is ... disturbing; it is even indecent, morbid or blasphemous, and therefore socially dangerous for the individual.'
C G Jung, Modern Man in Search of a Soul

3 Mental Illness & Community Context

Contents of this Chapter:

On a desert island inhabited by two or three people it would be impossible to have a dividing line between sanity and madness. There have to be a group of people, in order to have a measure for what passes for sanity.

If you have read part 1, you might recall the ship of fools, an early practice of sending insane people to sea in the hope of their finding a cure. Some of them were cured although others died in misery far from home. On such a ship, bearing in mind what I have said above are the patients or sailors insane? There will be more patients than sailors.

Key Learning 10 Diagnosis and Community
Diagnosis has little meaning outside community settings.

Commonality of Mental Illness

The prevalence of mental illness is surprisingly high, with nearly 25% of the population being liable to be diagnosed at some point in their lives; about the same number with that terrible scourge, depressive illness. Given this prevalence, the current tendency of stigmatisation is absurd.

I believe the overwhelming reason for stigmatisation is fear, due to lack of education about both mental illness and mental health. The Government have stipulated that mental health education is taught in schools but a quick glance at the new national curriculum shows that this is not being viewed as seriously as it might.

There are no standards, in citizenship nor health, to give teachers a guide to what should be taught. When I checked with the Department for Health and Education, I was told this was left to individual schools. This is a glaring omission.

****

Figure 3 Life Stress Factors: Burdens of Mental Illness

Key Learning 11 Commonality of Mental Illness
Current figures show a quarter of the population likely to become mentally ill during their lives.

I went further, in explaining that everyone experiences some phenomena which could be taken for symptoms of mental illness. I gave the examples of bereavement and falling in love both of which trigger extreme emotional reaction; that it was common for people to have hallucinations of dead people [if recently bereaved]. This is why clinicians, particularly new ones, have to exercise extreme caution when using clinical terminology which labels people.

Key Learning 12 Misinterpretation of Symptoms
It is easy to misperceive and therefore misinterpret symptoms.

Community and Mental Illness

I covered aspects of the links between community and mental illness in detail in the first book but will give a brief synopsis.

No one knows the cause of mental illness and probably we will never know because the issues are complex. However, it is generally accepted these factors are involved:

- environment – birth, living conditions
- genetics, parental behaviour
- psychological make-up
- cultural issues, personal beliefs
- life events
- community attitude - the acceptance factor

So you can see there are both internal and external factors and that some are set in stone [genetic factors] whilst others can alter [attitude and environment]. These factors do not work in isolation, but are linked e.g.:

- life events affect individual psychology
- environment has an effect on cultural issues.

Environment – We have no control about the conditions under which we are born; the area, class, parentage, relations, upbringing. However, as we grow up we begin to exercise choices as we separate from parental influences.

Some people have such traumatic early lives that it may take decades to recover, if they recover at all. For others, they will transcend life experience to live rich, full lives. Some might have been lucky enough to live wonderful lives but life events strike them later in life and [being unused to dealing with trauma] they collapse.

Genetics – Although the genetic code has been broken by Francis, Wilkins, Watson and Crick there is a long way to go before there is a deep understanding of the links between the genes and psychological makeup. We know the names of the proteins that are the building blocks of living matter and how they fit together, but we cannot predict what a person will grow up to become – how their life will turn out. This is the meaning of my poem Cradle Song.

Psychological make-up – this is a complex issue. There is not only the genetic [birth] factor but the complexities of how a person learns to communicate with the world because of:

- their experiences [life events – what happens to them]
- their perceptions [how they view their experiences].

This is sometimes referred to as the nature versus nurture argument; whether upbringing or genetics is responsible for the resulting psychological profile of a person. Where I find this most interestingly played out is in the psychological profiles of serial killers and bullies.

Cultural issues – I think we have all witnessed in recent news how far culture can affect individuals and large groups of people - for better or worse. This rivalry is played out on sports fields, so-called organised religions, gang warfare as well as more broadly in nations.

Supporting an individual view often comes at great cost both to the individual and the communities they live in. This is a constant battle; those who desire to live in peace and those who would thwart them; those open to change and zealots. There is no one more dangerous than someone with zeal however, there is also no one more prone to success than someone with an altruistic mission.

Life events – we cannot get away from life events; for better or for worse. Experience and our attitude towards it shapes our future. Our attitudes are linked with culture, genes and psychological makeup. I will go further and say serial killers and saints originate from the same source. More of that in another book.

Community attitude – I have experienced this at first hand; a community turning on someone and destroying them. Like tyrant children, some of our communities can be vituperative and destructive especially if ill informed or those types with no insight or control. I have also seen how individuals can rise above their circumstances.

Living with supportive people makes a difference to everyone particularly those with mental health problems.

Key Learning 13 Community Factors in Mental Illness
Many complex factors of living in communities can affect mental health; genes, other people, environment, culture, acceptance etc.

Living in Communities – Summing Up

Living in a community is not easy. Reading an individual's meaning is difficult – image the number of times you have made assumptions about someone, only for that view to be blown as you got to know the person. Multiply this factor by thousands, all with pathology, personal agendas and issues.

When you add mental illness into this murky soup the potential for damage is colossal, to the patient, their family and friends and the community at large.

****

Summary of Key Learning Points:

Key Learning 10 Diagnosis and Community
Diagnosis has little meaning outside community settings.

Key Learning 11 Commonality of Mental Illness
Current figures show a quarter of the population likely to become mentally ill during their lives.

Key Learning 12 Misinterpretation of Symptoms
It is easy to misperceive and therefore misinterpret symptoms.

Key Learning 13 Community Factors in Mental Illness
Many complex factors of living in communities can affect mental health; genes, other people, environment, culture, acceptance etc.

Figure 4 DNA: Cradle Song

Cradle Song

They say the secrets out, nothing left to know.
Franklin, Wilkins, Watson and Crick have written
The Book of Life, the definitive version.
DNA (The film of the book will soon be on its way).

2.9 billion letters and 100,000 proteins
In synthesis - that's life in a nutshell.
Even then, the scientists say,
It can be boiled down a bit more
To just four proteins;
'Adenine', 'Thymine', 'Cytosine' 'Guanine'.

Silent, the baby sleeps -
Tiny blank pages in an unwritten book.

Pale moonbeams slither on icy pavements
The frost shimmers like fragmented stars
The night-sky shivers in wispy robes of cloud.
As the womb-waters rocked, now the cradle rocks.

Child of your dreams, beloved son, cherished grandson.
Where will life take you? What will you become?
Adenine - the pioneer? Thymine - the scientist?
Cytosine - the artist? Guanine - the man of peace?
Womb to cradle. Cradle to ship. Ship's Captain.

All we can wish for you is a fair wind with full sails
And fine weather. A sound and loyal crew.
Your mother's love and care. Strong arms to hold you
And a wise heart to guide you. A port in the storm.
Adenine the pioneer; Thymine the scientist
Cytosine the artist, Guanine the man of peace.

Marianne Richards 2004

Figure 5 Living in Communities

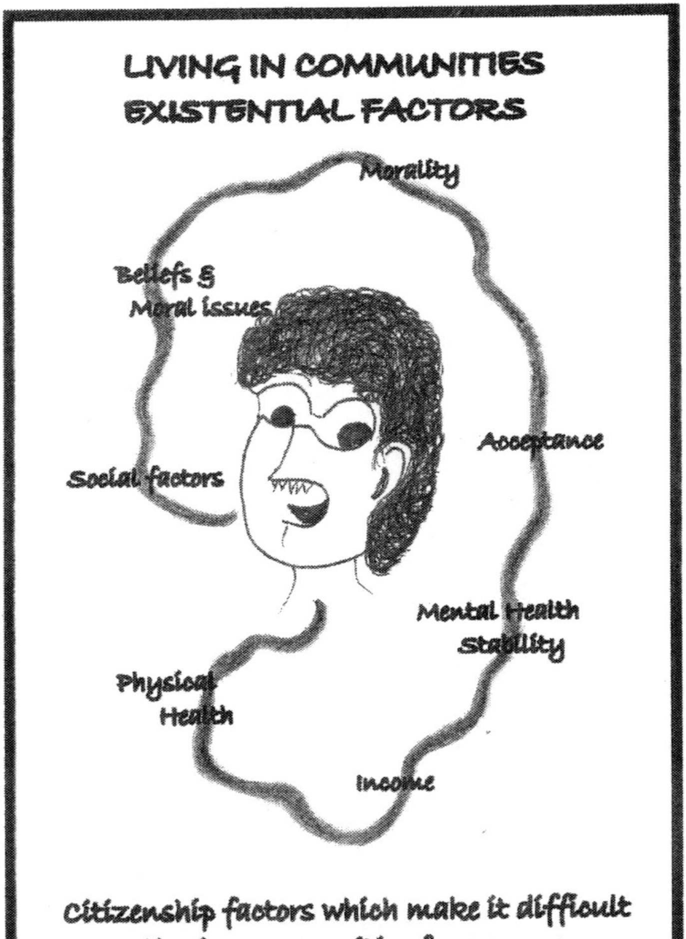

CASE STUDIES

'But it's not magic' [said Esk]
'most magic isn't.. it's .. knowing the.. ways of people'
Terry Pratchett, Equal Rites

4 Vignettes

Contents of this Chapter:

It is difficult for an author to predict how you, as a reader and student of mental health, will want to use a book for learning. There are many ways of presenting materials and it is not always easy to choose which you will enjoy and find useful.

I decided to present this material in several ways;

- narrative vignettes rather than case studies
- diagnoses of major mental illnesses based on DSM IV
- explanations for major factors; diagnosis, assessment, confidentiality etc
- illustrative diagrams

In my first series '**Understanding Mental Illness**' I covered a range of mental illnesses, showing DSMIV and case study equivalents. In a later version I added non-medical treatments with an informal diagnostic exercise. For this book, I decided to tackle it differently.

This chapter comprises a series of vignettes, such as might illuminate a particular symptom or illness. **Note:** these are not real people and in no particular order.

I have offered no commentary, diagnostic information nor notes as to specific diagnoses for each vignette. You can read the material and decide for yourself what, if anything, is amiss. This will give you practice in analysis of the problem.

You will find my suggested diagnoses for these vignettes at the end of the chapter on major mental illnesses.

Remember these vignettes are brief; and I have kept out the elaborate details which a patient will bring in a therapeutic session. I wanted to make it easier for you, whilst giving you a fair picture of what diagnosis and assessment are like.

****

It might be useful to **keep a bookmark in place at either end of this block of vignettes** so that you can refer back to them whilst reading the chapters on:

- medical treatments
- mainstream non medical
- alternative or complementary treatments.

****

Emma

"If I knew I had to go through this again, I would kill myself. I really believed 'they' were following me trying to control my mind. Everyone was in the plot even the doctor and my husband. It was a nightmare - only it was happening during the daytime.

I am 40 and was separated after 10 years of marriage. It was not happy. We had no children but looking back I think that was lucky because I would have hated children to go through all this.

My job was awful; a clerical job in a run down office of a housing charity. The Manager hated me and didn't he show it! Tried to get rid of me several times but a nice woman defended me, that is 'til he managed to get rid of her too. There was a drunk manager there too, and he made my life hell.

I can't remember how I ended up in hospital. I think it was Joe, one of my friends. He said I had ignored his calls so he came to my flat. The lights were out but he saw me moving around upstairs. The rest you know.

They asked me to describe it, but it was difficult. You know, the whole scenario was so real! I can't remember it coming on, I mean where it changed from me being sane to thinking there were these things in the house from space, trying to take over my mind.

They say that no one really remembers this, because it's where you lose insight into the fact that you are getting ill. It was sheer hell.

I don't remember how I recovered. I remember bits of reality coming back, as Joe brought bits and pieces to me from home – clothes, books or a few records. I realized that I was 'me' and the things I had thought real did not exist. That was the worst part at first, a real shock – not knowing what was real and what was this awful fantasy.

The worst bit was afterwards. I remember the police dragging me into their car and I was screaming. All the bloody neighbours were curtain twitching. That's why I didn't want to go back. Joe sold the place for me and I moved away in the end. I couldn't face the neighbours and the gossip."

****

Alicia

"I can't remember how it started, but it seemed to be going on for a long time. I was 56 and had been for counselling before but this time I had thought I could cope with Sam's illness.

I couldn't respond to friends, but all the time I was saying to myself 'for God's sake don't leave me alone'. Some of them couldn't stand it and deserted me which made it hard, because I started feeling guilty as well, which made it worse.

Mother had had this thing too but I hadn't realized it until I had it myself. She used to spend hours weeping but could never explain why or else she would lie in bed for hours on end, pretending to be asleep if any of us went into her room.

There was no medication nor any real help so God knows she must have suffered a hell of a lot. She tried to kill herself twice and that was awful for us kids. Father didn't know what to do. He left in the end but I suppose I can't blame him.

I don't know what it was with me, genes or my awful marriages. Mother had never been alert enough to be with me so I didn't learn the things a normal teenager would, neither did my sister. We both had several bad marriages and a string of awful boyfriends; nonces and scallywags. Same at work. Always seemed to be picked on.

I don't know what helped in the end. It might have been discovering painting. I know I feel happiest when painting or buying art stuff. I started to exhibit in galleries and gradually found a new life. I married Adrian a few years later. We have a quiet life; we both like that after all the years of trauma."

****

Joseph

"I don't know what mum is worried about. I eat more than any of my friends. Exercise? Yes. I go to the gym every day. If I don't, I feel I've missed out on something. How long? About three or four hours a night. Well, I don't think that's a bit much because some of the real serious guys, the weight lifters, do more than that".

Joseph is very slender with clearly defined muscles; you might say, too clearly defined. What you might notice about him on first sight are his large eyes which slightly dull giving him a sad appearance. Joseph has come to the clinic reluctantly because his parents are worried about him, but he thinks nothing is wrong.

It is a hot day but Joseph is wearing a hooded tracksuit top with at least two T-shirts underneath. When the doctor asks him if he wouldn't mind removing the top so that his blood pressure can be taken he reluctantly does so revealing abnormally thin, though muscular, arms.

"Why do you keep asking me about food? I mean, everyone is obsessed about it. What is it with all of you?" Joseph is clearly getting annoyed so the GP changes tack.

"School? Well, school wasn't that good. Some of the teachers were a bit rough. I'd rather not say about that but we were glad to leave. I don't know what I want. I started in a warehouse because mum needed me to earn something but I hate it. They take everything off you, keep on at you, you know, to do overtime. They dock you for lateness but don't say thanks when you're early or work over."

"Exams? Well, I did GCSEs. I liked sport and stuff but dad said that won't earn you a crust. Other things? Well, science was ok and maths. I found those easy. I sometimes helped my mates with their homework and they paid me in beer. No, I don't drink a lot. Hey can you leave out this stuff. You promised not to talk about food."

Joseph is edgy. The Doctor is anxious not to appear threatening because the boy might walk out. This has happened to him before.

The Doctor holds up his hands and tells Joseph not to shoot. Joseph laughs and as he does, the Doctor notices the mottled, yellow teeth, with two front ones missing. He makes a note but doesn't say anything.

"'No one's asked me what I like before. What? No, not even at school. The teachers didn't like me. They said I was disruptive. I don't know what they meant but I used to get a laugh in class, you know something the teacher said. No, I wasn't happy. I think I was playing clown. Well, sometimes I get a bit down and well, I don't want to talk about it. Is that all? I gotta go."

The Doctor realizes Joseph is getting edgy so he asks if he will come back to see him and have another chat. Joseph says he will, as long as he doesn't mention food again. The Doctor says it is a deal and Joseph laughs again.

****

Thelma

"It's not me at all, but like a bizarre character from a film. There's no warning, well perhaps a slight feeling of unreality as if everything has got more colour.

Every time the pattern is more or less the same. I seem to get into this character that I call her Ameltha because she's a kind of

Thelma turned inside out. Ameltha does things that I wouldn't dream of doing."

Thelma is shy and mousy. A typical librarian type with round glasses and traditional, sensible clothing with flat shoes. Her hair is long and wound into a tight bun. She wears a little makeup but you can tell she is ill. Her eyes are surrounded by dark shadows and her face is too pale.

She nervously pulls at threads on her coat. It takes several weeks to get the whole story out. Some weeks she doesn't arrive at the surgery for her appointment and I wonder where she is, what she is doing, who she is being at any given time.

"About six months ago, I started drawing money out of my savings account and putting it in a tin under the bed. It went on for a few weeks. I hadn't been well for a while but no one had noticed because I live alone and my two best friends were away on holiday in Tunisia.

I took nearly all of it, nearly £10,000 to a casino in that large hotel [xxx]. I dressed up in this red satin suit and high-heeled shoes. They were all looking because it left nothing to the imagination. I stayed there all night, drinking and chatting the men up. And of course" [she lowered her voice and started to cry] "I took a couple of them up to my room."

Thelma burst into tears and was sobbing for over half an hour. I didn't interrupt her. She was exhausted. She started again in a very hesitant voice.

"I mean, the money was bad enough but [name withheld] was worse. You see, it wasn't technically rape because I was encouraging them, or Ameltha was. The things they did! I was being Ameltha and it seemed ok at the time. I thought I was in control of them, using them. But they were using me. I suppose they look out for women like Ameltha".

I examine her. She has the typical bruising on her legs and inner thighs. She is torn and I have to stitch her up. There are bite marks on her face, neck and shoulders. There are burn marks on her wrists and ankles. I may be a GP but I caught my breath when I saw the scarring on her back and buttocks.

"I can't go to the police. What would I say? As far as I know, there no law that covers it. They would say I consented. Oh yes, I know I could call a Psychiatrist in evidence but what good would that do? I would lose my job and my respect."

She is a professional with a good job, respected, a church goer. No one knows about Ameltha not even her two close friends. She laughs and my blood runs cold. That laugh! She is close to the edge.

"Ameltha is ruining me. I can't control her, it." She starts to scream and then fits. I call the nurse and give her an injection to calm her while I call the hospital. The doctor injects her and calls the hospital. She is sectioned.

[A few years later, she is referred to me again.]

I ask if she has is still taking Lithium. In response, she holds out her hands. They are trembling. Parkinsonism. Lithium prescriptions are wrecking her nervous system. I ask aloud why else she won't use it because I know that for weeks on end she doesn't.

"It is as if I am nothing without Ameltha. That my life doesn't count. No one notices me. She gives me something, a kind of edge, even though I know the consequences. It's like a drug, this mood. It's as if life suddenly has meaning, that I am the centre rather than being on the tail end. I think that, for a minute or two, I can control the moods but it takes over.

I get this feeling of power and confidence but I get frightened and want to back out but it's too late. Ameltha's off to a club. My savings are gone. The house is to be re-possessed. I don't know what to do. My life is not worth living."

[two weeks later, she commits suicide].

****

Lesley

Lesley was cleaning the corners of the window frame with a toothbrush when I arrived. I saw her face from the other side of the window, anxious, red-eyed, almost unaware of her actions. She took a while to answer the door, but when she did, she still had the toothbrush in her hand.

Her husband had called the service. He had tried to stop her after several hours but she was still scrubbing away at the imaginary dirt. I could tell he had had enough; he had that look in his eyes. This cleaning had been going on for years and it had worn him down too. I think she realized and that is why she agreed to see me.

It wasn't as if Lesley appeared to have any problems. Nice house, loving husband, two children at University. She had no money worries. Her childhood had been normal and she was higher than average intelligence. She had told me this a year or more ago. She seemed puzzled at her own behaviour.

"I've tried to stop. Of course I want to. Why do you think I want my fingers to bleed like this? I love Geoff and I know what he is thinking. I don't know what I would do if he left. I know if it doesn't stop that he might."

She picks up a cloth and starts wiping the windowpane, mechanically. "'It's no good asking me why. If I knew that, I wouldn't do it. What do I get out of it? Well, the room will be cleaner when I've finished." We both laugh and that breaks the tension.

"I just feel, well, if I don't do it then Geoff and the kids will think I'm being a slob. I don't want that. But it's more than that. I start to feel anxious, stressed really and as soon as I pick up a cloth or duster there's a sort of relief, a calmness comes over me."

The calmness doesn't last more than a minute or two. By then she has started the whole procedure over; top to bottom, the whole house. She can't stop, feels forced to complete her ritual.

If she misses a bit, she starts again. Most of the day is taken over with it. She doesn't socialise. Her world is narrowed to this perfectly clean, tidy house she sees as grubby and untidy.

****

Simon

"I wish I knew how it started. It seems ridiculous, especially for a man like me." He chews his fingernail thoughtfully, rapping the fingers of his free hand on his left knee.

We are sitting in his cottage, in one of those idyllic villages you see in photographs. He laughed when I said this would be the worst place for him to live in these circumstances. He gestures, encompassing the entire cottage it seems.

"My father's legacy. Nearly half a million. I can't let it go. The property market's depressed."

I asked him if it was that important, money over his mental state. He laughed again but this time it was a cynical laugh. He was moderately wealthy, somewhat of a playboy and a shrewd businessman. He would bring secretaries and other girls down here at weekends when his wife was away.

I saw him anxiously eyeing beams, cracks in the woodwork. "At night", he said, "it's worse at night. I'm not afraid of anything, but.." His voice tailed off.

He was not the sort of man you would want to see on a dark night, I mused. He had a vague air of something not quite pukka. But he had a problem and I had to cast aside my own feelings and try to help.

"So, what is it?" I said after a while.

"It's down to shapes now" he said. "Even cracks in the wall. Some of them have fissures. They look like.."

"Spider legs?" I ventured.

He stared at me, eyes narrowing. White-knuckle fear. I could tell he was terrified of losing something else; his reason. It didn't add up for him, how such a small thing can raise terror in a normal, hard headed businessman.

To most people it would seem strange, laughable, for such a man to be afraid of spiders. Some things are not easily explainable in rational terms but nevertheless they exist. You need to remember, the mind is a powerful machine but with dangerous undercurrents.

****

Sandy

Maude and Arthur are sitting next to me on the threadbare sofa. They are theatricals, film extras with speaking walk-on parts here and there. They make a reasonable living because they are good at what they do. Their daughter Sandy is a worry to them and taints their peace of mind.

She was diagnosed with schizophrenia when she was 16 and at art school. A talented girl, she was expected to follow family tradition in the creative arts. Now, two years later, she is living a shadowy life in an inner city bedsit, rarely allows visits from her parents or by Social Worker she dislikes [he made the mistake of laughing at her drawings of hallucinatory figures].

"She was always a friendly girl, loved animals, loved her art and drawing. I remember she made a sculpture of her pet dog when she was seven – remember that Arthur?"

Arthur nods but remains silent, sitting in his armchair sad eyed and quiet. He loves his pretty daughter, was delighted when she got a place at Art College and can't understand what has happened to her; why she gave up Art college and is unemployed and depressed. He can't take in what any of the professionals tell him, particularly when they say there is no cure. He can't get beyond the words 'no cure'.

"We bought her a car to help her become independent, but are worried about her driving. We have to keep hoping that she will go back to the Unit if she feels unwell. What if she doesn't take her medication and those things come on?"

'Those things' are the hallucinations; frightening visions and voices which terrify Sandy. Once, she attacked her father with a chisel cutting his arm so badly he lost the use of several fingers. They refused to press charges even though the policewoman felt it would help; that the Courts might give an order so that she received better care.

"She's still my girl" Arthur suddenly says, with fierce pride, "she'll find a way through. Made of steel my Sandy." He still thinks of the other Sandy, the confident girl, not the one who is living in a twilight, dreamscape world where nightmare and reality are mixed together.

Maude sighs and squeezes Arthur's arm. "I just don't like the thought of her living up there. I know she can scream and rage and break things when she has delusions but at least we can keep an eye on her. I worry that she doesn't eat properly. She likes her grub, my Sandy." She stifles a sob and Arthur turns to her, kissing her gently on the forehead.

They are getting older now, a loving couple who had high hopes for their daughter only to be shattered by this, the most devastating of all illnesses. They cannot be sure she is taking vital anti-psychotic medication and are afraid of a relapse.

They look at her photograph in a silver frame, and start to talk about her younger days. Arthur brightens as he joins in.

As they sit there together, under the yellow light from their standard lamps, I can see them as they once were; when they had been a proper family and enjoyed normal family life. I cannot help but feel their loss.

****

Soraya

Soraya is a 30-year old Indian girl. Her family moved to the UK when she was a baby. Apart from the odd holiday they have never returned to the home of their ancestors. However, they still adhere to their culture and beliefs, difficult though it has been for Soraya to accept.

Soraya is Westernised and has always attended Western schools. She was brought up to respect her culture but not forced to follow the Muslim faith. She wears Western clothing but keeps her legs covered in the traditional way, more because she is shy and modest than out of tradition.

She hoped to find an English boyfriend but her parents forbade it and she daren't disobey. She is afraid of her father and uncles who keep a close watch on her.

For several years since she moved away from home, Soraya has lived alone in a large flat in the suburbs of a city. She has a good job in a bank which earns her a good living. She has plenty of spare cash to spend and could easily go out but chooses to spend much of her time in her flat, where she feels safe and comfortable.

Soraya is a worry to her few friends from the bank. She has been to some of their functions and spends her lunch hour with the women, but has never invited any of them to her flat. From what she tells them, Soraya spends a lot of her time reading or watching movies on TV. She is a kind girl but naïve.

Lately, she has been giving a lot of money to charitable causes and wears brighter clothing than usual. She is starting to argue world events with colleagues during lunch hours but before she would sit and eat her food in silence.

They have noticed she is eating meat. She was vegetarian but now she eats chicken legs, chops and mixed grills from a takeaway around the corner from the bank

Janice, one of her closest colleagues, is concerned. Soraya became angry over something someone said in the canteen and hit the girl with her handbag, burst into tears and rushed out into the street. The men found it funny but Soraya's colleagues were surprised.

Janice, a Supervisor, told Markus the Bank Manager about these things. She felt it was out of character for Soraya. He told her confidentially that Soraya was starting to make mistakes in her work, which was unusual.

They wondered if Soraya had a medical problem, perhaps some kind of brainstorm. They didn't know what to do and were guessing. Janice suggested they call Soraya in for a chat.

****

QUALITY: EVIDENCE & DIAGNOSIS

'it is better to learn wisdom late, than not at all'
Conan Doyle, The Man with the Twisted Lip

'Experience.. is the comb life gives you when you no longer have hair'
Mavis Cheek, Mrs Fytton's Country Life

5 Evidence: Experiment v Experience

Contents of this Chapter:

Quality Control in Therapies
About Medical, Complementary & Alternatives
Lack of Funding
National Institute for Health & Clinical Excellence [NICE]
Social Care Centre for Excellence [SCIE]
Evidence Base in Primary Care
The Need for Research
Therapeutic Relationship and Placebo
Medication in Mental Health

In this chapter, I will briefly cover the regulatory machinery of medical and therapeutic treatments, which ensure that:

- Patients are not cheated
- Standards are maintained
- New treatments are tested and approved
- Therapists practice in an ethical manner

I have called the chapter 'experiment v experience' because there are two main ways in which we can find out if things work [are effective]:

- **Experiment** – research
- **Experience** – by doing or receiving the treatment

Western medicine tends to be based on experiment whilst Eastern medicine values experience. None of these are the correct way; it depends upon what is being tested.

If potentially dangerous chemicals are being concocted in a laboratory for consumption by the public then there needs to be legislation for its manufacture and a license. Research has to be carried out on the chemicals, practitioners prescribing need to be regulated, the drug has to be licensed for sale under specific conditions.

If patients are being offered therapeutic services like healing or counselling there need to be ethical guidelines in place to ensure the patient is treated with respect. Therapeutic practice needs to be underpinned through training.

It is true that, pre-umbrella days, practitioners were happily practicing on the basis of long experience with patients. Their effectiveness proven by the fact they remained in business! This is still the case in many alternative treatments.

The field of talking cures is relatively new and still being regulated – one hopes it will not become over-regulated as some organisations have become.

On the other hand, training is no assurance of effectiveness, ethics or quality. I have experienced both sides of this coin; individuals clearly were well qualified but lacked basic life nous.

I covered, in the first book of this series, the mental health legislation which underpins treatment of seriously ill patients in the community. However, the following refers to patients, service users, clients – call them what you will – who voluntarily choose to take treatment privately or on the NHS.

Key Learning 14 Evidence v Experience

There are two ways of learning about clinical matters; evidence [research, science] and experience [working with patients].

Quality Control in Therapies

In all purchased services we have forms of quality control to make sure customers are not cheated and goods are kept up to standard.

In ancient medical history quality control may well have meant the priest Ugg being clubbed to death or Inzar the priestess being buried alive by angry mobs if their rituals were not effective.

Nowadays there are statutory and voluntary bodies acting on the punters behalf in marginally less vindictive ways for example:

- Government public health regulations
- National Institute for Health & Clinical Effectiveness [who use the quaint acronym NICE]
- Social Care Institute for Excellence [SCIE]
- legislative instruments [policy]
- British Medical Association
- Mind, the mental health charity
- Carers UK

We also all have free access to courts and as a last resort to local and national media, as well as professional umbrella associations. By the latter I do not mean purveyors of rain protective equipment but organisations which represent the different schools within the professions.

Each profession has its own umbrella [e.g. British Association for Counselling, which covers counselling and Psychotherapy].

Unfortunately for you, there are so many of these bodies and associations that it is virtually impossible to know about all of them. What happens mostly is that you learn about the ones you need and some others filter in through the media, contacts and research.

About Medical, Complementary & Alternatives

Thanks to patient demand, mainstream medicine [as far as this book is concerned, NHS and Primary Care] is being forced to look at areas once scorned by stuffy traditionalists.

The term medical is generally used for invasive treatments such as drugs, ECT or surgery. The trade of nursing is usually bundled in this area as nurses administer drugs but some mental nurses dispute this grouping and claim their theories are entirely separate from the medical model.

The terms complementary and alternative are used interchangeably but there is a difference. Complementary is usually taken to be in addition to medical treatment whereas alternative therapists operate outside the medical system in their own right.

Do not take these differentials as gospel truth because the degree of overlap also depends on the stance of individual practitioners. A therapist spending 5 or more years training with a great deal of patient experience does not want to feel that all their patients have to visit a GP first, which is I am sure, what the Government would ultimately like.

In Primary Care, where Doctors are starting to offer patients choice over treatment, certain alternatives are now accepted:

- massage therapy
- osteopathy
- acupuncture
- herbal medicine
- homoeopathy

I described some better-known complementary treatments in **Understanding Mental Illness.**

Complementary and alternative medicine is big business and you will finds hundreds of variations from the logical to the downright insane. One of the most bizarre so-called therapeutic objects I have seen is a wire copper pyramid, which would be purchasers place over their head. There is some notion about pyramids being centres of healing, based on an urban myth about the pyramids in Egypt.

Expensive manufactured items should be purchased after a great deal of caution and certainly not while the judgement is clouded, for example whilst in an emotional or traumatic state.

Alternative therapists treat on a holistic basis; balancing the three elements of mind, body and spirit. This is logical – do you feel better when stressed in a busy place or when on holiday? The holiday represents the spiritual element or getting away from it all as we say.

With growing demand for holistic treatment attitudes are changing in the NHS and gradually alternatives are coming on board. There are even trad. Nurses setting up anti-smoking clinics based on hypnotic techniques.

Later in this chapter I will describe the work of SCIE, who are the equivalent of NICE and are being funded for values based research in social care treatments.

Social research is moving away from traditional research [measures or quantitative research] into an equally scientific method of measuring values, quality of life and ethics [qualitative research].

However funding is slow so don't hold onto your hat hoping your favourite treatment will eventually be recognised [as has my therapeutic form, brief therapy, nearly a decade after I qualified – reader, you have to be lucky sometimes!]

Key Learning 15 Changing Styles of Treatment
The NHS is starting to accept alternative and complementary treatments, as patients exercise choice away from trad medicine.

Lack of Funding

The Government has little funding for research projects although their ideal is complete regulation [hence, control over] all treatments. Over-regulation is not always for the right reasons, i.e. best care of patients.

Traditional medicine and therapies have regulatory bodies, training and umbrella organisations springing up all over the place. These often have large numbers of staff in grand buildings and charge phenomenal membership fees.

This system excludes good therapists, particularly those on minimum wage rates. They either have to give up their career dreams or work at several other jobs at the same time as practicing therapy. Although we do not like to acknowledge the class system I'm afraid it still exists in this therapeutic class ceiling and is to do with income not pre-ordained status.

As more and more therapies are regulated, this squeezes out smaller but excellent training schools who cannot afford the large fees demanded by umbrella organisations.

Key Learning 16 The Class Ceiling in Therapy
There is a class ceiling in the therapies, due to the extortionate cost of training, professional development and supervision.

The Government is already in talks with the BAC to try to make counselling less elitist, by reducing their onerous training requirements for accreditation. The costs of supervision, rooms and insurance is so onerous that counsellors have to charge business-like rates. Even NHS Primary Care is getting in on the act, with high room hire rates being charged by cash strapped Practice Managers who are thus unwittingly adding to the problematic situation.

Unfortunately, this situation at the end of the day means that patients who need counselling are unable to find affordable treatment.

Key Learning 17 Why No Affordable Therapy?
Training and cost are at the heart of the ongoing problem of lack of affordable therapy for Primary Care patients.

National Institute for Health & Clinical Excellence [NICE]

The National Institute for Health and Clinical Excellence [NICE] is an organisation set up as a result of the 2004 white paper, Choosing Health: Making Health Choices Easier.

The Government wanted to bring together knowledge and guidance on promoting good health, as well as treating ill health. Like the Government, NICE uses independent advisory groups, comprised of both professionals and lay people who have an interest in or experience of mental health issues.

NICE offers guidance on clinical practice and the use of new and existing medicines and treatments in the NHS. The Department of Health refer specific health issues to NICE, who then look at the evidence and develop recommendations for [for example] the use of medications or preparations intended for patient prescriptions in Primary Care.

Clinical guidelines are a form of standard which ensure treatments that work are offered to patients. For example, Cognitive Behavioral Therapy and Brief Therapy [solution focused] have been ratified by NICE as treatments of choice in Primary Care for patients with depressive illness.

NICE, like all NHS organisations, has limited funds and so resources are scarce. Funds are spent on developing guidelines on conditions that affect large groups of people, such as depression and anxiety or which have a significant impact on the health of the population, such as obesity.

For social care, there is an equivalent organisation called the Social Care Institute for Excellence [SCIE].

Social Care Centre for Excellence [SCIE]

Unlike NICE, SCIE enjoys charitable status and is therefore independent of the Government, although it was set up by them in 2001, to improve how social care is delivered, by offering good practice guidance.

SCIE is supported by the Department of Health as well as the Department for Education and Skills [DfES] and is run by a Board of Trustees. There are two main organisational arms:

The Partners' Council

The Partners' Council comprises some 40 organisations that are connected with health issues [e.g. patient, carer, research institutes] who advise SCIE on priority issues

The Practice Partners' Network

The Practice Partners Network has a circle of member organisations from all three statutory, voluntary and private sectors, who share experiences on good practice.

Figure 6 SCIE's Services

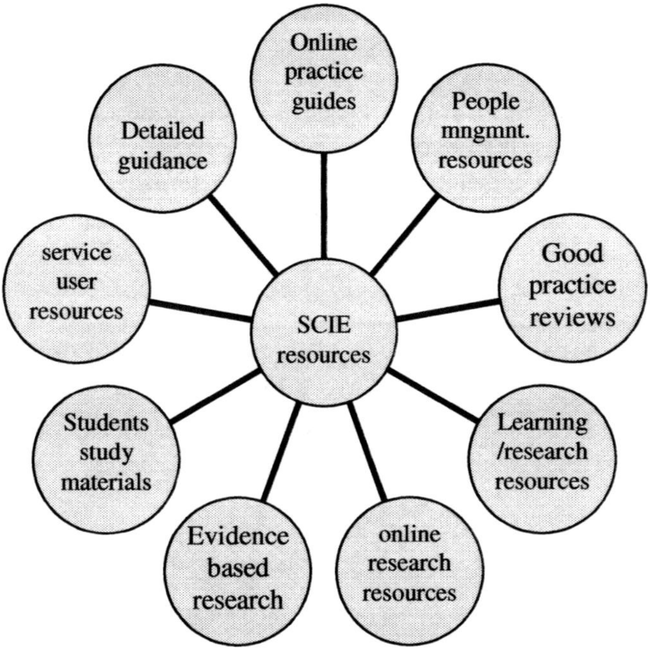

Key Learning 18 Evidence Based Care
The two main NHS bodies responsible for gathering evidence bases for care are NICE and SCIE.

Evidence Base in Primary Care

Whilst researching NICE and SCIE I found an interesting website; the Somerset Trust for Integrated Healthcare, which I thought you might be interested in.

These alternatives were offered to patients who had muscular pains but more particularly, for social and emotional distress. The results were very positive, showing that [quote]

> 'cost-savings had been achieved through a reduction of referrals to secondary care and a reduction in usage of

other health services (GP time, prescriptions, X-rays and other tests)'.

The Need for Research

As I mentioned earlier, little money is being diverted to research into treatments outside conventional medicine, so it is refreshing to find small-scale research like the Somerset project being carried out in the very heart of Primary Care. And it also demonstrates there are research funds to be had, albeit it seems you have to make a great deal of effort to find them. A challenge you will take up, I hope!

So, what other factors do we need to consider around the area of treatments before we dive into the nitty-gritty of details? One is the surprising but often forgotten facts around basic premises which are used [sometimes exploited by] practitioners –

- therapeutic relationship
- placebo effect
- hope

These three have long been known to medics.

Therapeutic Relationship and Placebo

'The belief, the self-confidence, perhaps also the devotion with which the analyst does his work, are far more important to the patient ... than the rehearsing of old traumata' C G Jung

The therapeutic relationship should not be undervalued. It is recognised as a vital process in therapy as is the patient's belief system.

In my book **Understanding Mental Illness**, I described how there is always a blind trial within drug trials, where some participants are given an inert substance instead of the drug being tested. This is to ensure benefits of the drug cannot be ascribed to patient belief [what is called the placebo effect].

The link between patient belief and cure is fascinating and needs research. It is accepted by physicians that positive therapeutic relationship and placebo effect both have a bearing on successful outcomes. Another word you might use for placebo is hope.

A Channel 4 programme by Dr Kathy Sykes explored this in depth. During laying-on-of-hands healing sessions, CAT scans showed the patients pain centres visibly diminishing.

This demonstrates the physical benefit of the therapeutic relationship between healer and patient, whether you believe it is the relationship itself or some invisible and as yet unknown healing force within the person of the healer.

Key Learning 19 Therapeutic Relationship, Placebo, Hope
These topics are all related to empathy and belief; both powerful known healing qualities.

Medication in Mental Health

I explored the process of drug trials in Understanding Mental Illness. It takes up to a decade for a new drug to progress from first discovery to being made available to the public. This may shorten as virtual trials [computer simulation] start to become feasible.

Psychiatric drugs are a relatively new innovation, around the 1950's. Some of the earliest were:

- **Largactil** in syrup form - reduces psychotic symptoms
- **Anti depressants** – raises mood in depressive illness
- **Lithium** - levels the mood in mania
- **Haloperidol** – used in the treatment of psychosis

The discovery of anti-depressants is interesting and a good example of serendipity [where a discovery is made through coincidence]. Nurses on tuberculosis wards discovered that certain drugs were making their patients jubilant. Around the same time, work was being done by scientists on chemical transmitters in the brain, and how these affected mood levels.

Some insightful scientists started to put these facts together, and eventually the drugs which were being used for treating tuberculosis were synthesised into anti-depressants.

By the 1960's, the tranquillisers Librium and Valium were commonly prescribed [particularly to women] for nervous disorders until they were withdrawn from general use when they were found to be addictive.

Anti-depressant medication is commonly used for anxiety disorders. Prozac became very popular in the treatment of depression. Later, the SSRI class drugs fell from grace when the drugs regulatory authorities started investigations that a side effect was increasing suicidal ideation [though pharmaceutical giants Lilley, who produced Prozac, denied this].

Many people do not like synthesised [laboratory made] medication and prefer natural remedies, despite the fact that there is only anecdotal evidence for many natural remedies. St John's Wort is one of the better known remedies used for relieving the symptoms of depression and is now commonly available in pharmacies.

Key Learning 20 Medication in Mental Illness
Medication is widely used in major mental illness to alleviate symptoms such as psychosis, mania, depression. Such areas do not readily respond to talking cures.

****

Summary of Key Learning Points:

Key Learning 14 Evidence v Experience
There are two ways of learning about clinical matters; evidence [research, science] and experience [working with patients].

Key Learning 15 Changing Styles of Treatment
The NHS is starting to accept alternative and complementary treatments, as patients exercise choice away from trad medicine.

Key Learning 16 The Class Ceiling in Therapy
There is a class ceiling in the therapies, due to the extortionate cost of training, professional development and supervision.

Key Learning 17 Why No Affordable Therapy?
Training and cost are at the heart of the ongoing problem of lack of affordable therapy for Primary Care patients.

Key Learning 18 Evidence Based Care
The two main NHS bodies responsible for gathering evidence bases for care are NICE and SCIE.

Key Learning 19 Therapeutic Relationship, Placebo, Hope
These topics are all related to empathy and belief; both powerful known healing qualities.

Key Learning 20 Medication in Mental Illness
Medication is widely used in major mental illness to alleviate symptoms such as psychosis, mania, depression. Such areas do not readily respond to talking cures.

'How can one see the beauty of the day, when the mind and the heart and the brain are so clouded by the past as authority' Krishnamurti

6 A Personal Learning Journey

Contents of this Chapter:

I thought I would end this section with a few personal thoughts on my journey of discovery, trying to understanding mental illness in context.

On Learning

I remember being told as a teenager, by a very wise teacher, that experience is the best teacher. I always remembered this though I did not realize its implication until years later. I really value my life as a tool of learning however much I crave to be a real academic.

I am a butterfly learner. This is good in one sense, because it means I can surprise people with my broad base of interests. When I have a fascination for a subject, as I do mental health, I gather information from all kinds of sources; thinking outside the teacup and taking pleasure in finding obscure information not typically associated with the prime subject.

I was delighted when I started University at 52. I yearned to be a proper scientist rather than feeling a bit of an outsider; due to my lack of academic confidence. Several years ago I read about Einstein, deducing the theory of relativity by imagining himself riding on a sunbeam.

Scientists HAVE to be creative in order to create the hypothesis which precedes their experiment or research. I was then able to link my creative ability with my analytical self.

I think I want to say to you, do not despair if you do not consider yourself deeply intellectual - we ALL add value because of who we are, what we have done and how we apply these experiences.

Why Do We Become Analytical? One Answer!

I believe people from dysfunctional childhood backgrounds naturally become analytical or curious. We want to know the why and what, because it is comforting and makes the world feel safer. This trait is a lifelong habit - and it is a good one.

I've experienced episodic depressive illness since childhood. Although there were few clinical episodes, depression has coloured my thinking and affected my energy levels for decades.

I don't think many people, even doctors, realize how far the effect travels across the psyche and how long lasting it is. It has far reaching implications, including loss of social contact so vital for learning hidden social rules. My own lack of social contact was exacerbated both by my depression and a mild autistic spectrum disorder, known as Aspergers. However, it was these very life problems that gave me the mental space to develop my talents and interests.

It was common in the 1950's for childhood depression not to be recognised. I know my parents considered me lazy, abstruse and aloof and my peers did not accept me. I was often bullied because other children tend to do this to people who are perceived as different. In fact, I was often tired, highly anxious and lonely. I did not care to share this fact with others, because I learned that if you share your ideas and feelings, people often bully you more. This is a common experience I have often come across in many patients.

Years before I started working in the field, even before I knew what mental illness was, I studied people by reading mythology. This was at a very early age when most children were playing games or joining clubs. I suppose my rationale was that if I could understand what was happening in the world, I would understand how it operated:

- I would lose my fear of going mad [aged 6, I heard my mother being told my aunt was mad]
- I would be able to control my world
- I would understand my inner world

Later, when I started to fight off depression, I noticed I could control my mood if I caught it at the right point in the cycle. The episodes gradually started to shift further apart.

Commonality of Experience

When I came into the field as a trainee I started talking to colleagues, trainers, patients about their life experience and realized that most people have some kind of mental problem. I do not necessarily mean severe mental illness but anything from mild anxiety, obsessions or tendency to moodiness.

It was a revelation and a relief. Although it seemed obvious to others I was not in a minority, I lacked the education to know this myself. This is why I am determined to share my knowledge and take the risk of revealing my inner-self.

Overleaf Figure 7 Continuum Mental Health to Illness

Figure 7 Continuum - Mental Health to Illness

See overleaf

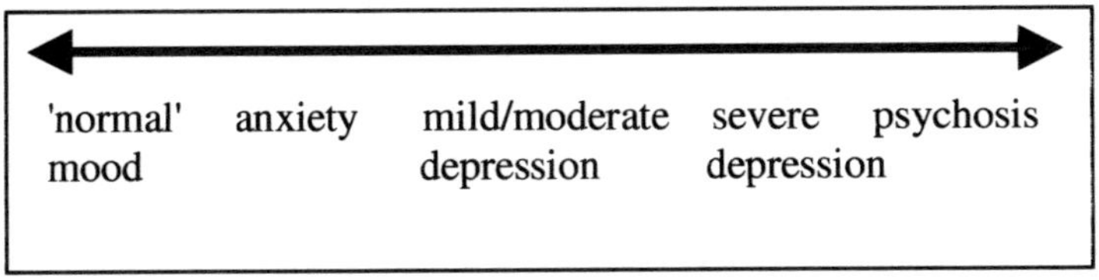

When I learned about the continuum theory of mental illness this confirmed that my thinking was right. Everyone has the potential to become mentally ill, and everyone will be anxious about something.

Notice I have drawn the scale with a double-headed arrow. This is to demonstrate that even at the far end of the scale there is a way back to normality [whatever normal means].

Key Learning 21 The Continuum Scale

See diagram. Mental illness is on a continuum with mental health – we all fit somewhere along this sliding scale, which moves as life events touch us.

I began to wonder where my peculiar experiences were coming from [that is to say, psychotic experiences when clinically depressed]. Surely if I no longer regarded myself as an isolated subspecies but a normal human being, what were these disturbances to perception about?

I began to read avidly about human experience, watch serious documentaries, order obscure books from the library [how patient those librarians were!] and scan internet sites. I was fascinated by world religion, mythology, archaeology, anthropology, serious crime and detection.

I wanted to understand the human mind. Never having been a social animal this was a difficult task. How could I observe people, though not necessarily being in close quarters with them? There were many answers:

- Books

- The Internet - specialist interest groups
- e-newsletters and journals
- my special interest groups
- mythology and other ethnographic study
- watching colleagues interact
- café watching [wear dark glasses in the summer and you can observe people very clearly!]

From such people-watching observations, it became clear that the spectrum of what passes for normal is wide ranging. Most people consider themselves normal yet at the same time they want to be considered unique.

Key Learning 22 Humans Crave to be Different!
It is a peculiarity of our species that we hate being isolated through differences, while not wanting to run with the wolf pack!

This is a long process of discovery, a life-long journey which is at times frustrating, exhilarating, painful and sometimes existentially lonely.

Mirrors to Daily Life

I started to consider, in the last 5 years, that the symptoms of mental illness resemble things that happen to us in daily life. That is why, although mental illness can be frightening, it is also a humanising experience.

I would like to demonstrate this briefly by looking at some of these parallel experiences. That is not to say I am taking away the enormity and suffering of mental illness – this is also a fact; however, the more we can understand it in terms of the everyday, the less stigma will attach itself to these conditions.

Take a look at the diagram on the next page, in which I have tried to make some parallels between everyday experiences and the symptoms of some of the mental illnesses. It is not an easy thing to do and I hope to refine the process as I update these books.

Figure 8 Parallel Experiences to Mental Illness Symptoms

Symptom	Experience
[in OCD] checking & testing	have you ever left your home, then had a feeling you had forgotten to lock your front door or switch off the oven? Doing this once or even twice could be considered 'normal'. In Obsessive compulsive disorder [OCD] such checking is continuous.
despair of depression	The depth of isolation you would experience during a bereavement, or loss of a deep love, mirror the isolation in depression.
[mania] Euphoria / exhaustion	There is an emotional overload and exhaustion connected with the experience of any fantastically happy event; marrying, having a child, even a cup final. But imagine going through this euphoria, outside your control, for days or weeks at a time. No matter how wonderful we think this would be, in fact no one can cope with such emotional overload. In mania, euphoria is out of control and eventually becomes frightening, with thoughts and actions following on so fast that mind and body are overwhelmed and become exhausted.
visual hallucination	Seeing or even physically feeling people you have loved is common after bereavement. If no one has told you this, it can be very frightening. Imagine that you were told, that the people you had been seeing were not real, but hallucinations?
auditory hallucination	Have you ever half heard something unpleasant about yourself, which you heard by accident? Imagine hearing voices criticising you, when there is no one around. Disembodied voices are frightening experiences, even if they are not 'saying' very obnoxious things.
psychosis - (paranoia)	Do you recall the worst nightmare you had, which re-occurred when you woke and went to sleep again?

	In psychoses, the nightmare experiences continue day and night until medication or exhaustion bring them to a halt.
depression	imagine the shock of bad news; a death in the family or a bad accident – the surreal quality of being unable to take it in. This shock and inertia mirrors the helplessness and isolation of depression.

Whilst the parallel experience theory is this is not an earth-shattering original discovery, it was pleasing to me when I read that others held the same view.

Key Learning 23 Find Parallel Experiences
As an exercise, after reading up on symptoms, see if you can think of any parallel experiences of your own, which will help you understand how a patient might be experiencing life.

What Do Mental Health Worker's Do?

I remember asking this rhetorical question many years ago, when I entered the field. I guess the answer has not changed that much. Although formal direction and qualifications were lacking, the truth upon which we based our work was to enable anyone with active mental illness to live fulfilled lives in the community. How that was to be achieved was another thing altogether.

I remember feeling quite lost until I started reading and studying for myself. It was one thing helping someone fill in housing or benefit forms, listening to relationship problems and existential life problems, quite another to help a stranger find their way towards existential fulfilment.

You can go on courses, listen to colleagues and supervisors, read extensively, but it will only start to make sense if you have experienced and overcome major problems in your own life and I don't necessarily mean mental illness [although it is my belief this is prerequisite for any depth of understanding].

So, although I can't describe what you are meant to do in your daily work, I offer you some of my own rules.

Some Informal Rules For Mental Health Workers

Reflection and Personal Experience

One cannot divorce life experience from practice; to do so would be folly. It is the ability to reflect and distance oneself from this experience that makes the difference.

Listen to the Patient's story

Do not bandy clinical terms or label people. How would you feel if someone called you a depressive for example. Try to understand your patient's situation; environment, culture and personal beliefs. Don't label someone as mentally ill just because they behave differently to your expectations.

Don't Put Up with Jargon

Jargon has its place, in being a kind of shorthand. However, it can be used to baffle or control rather than aid understanding. Some people use jargon because they think it sounds grand. It doesn't. Anyone who can't explain in simple terms does not understand the subject themselves.

Equality

There needs to be an equal relationship between therapist and patient. There is truly something wrong with a professional who demands a power differential.

Be Cautious of Taking Credit

If you take credit for what goes right, you need to accept blame for what goes wrong. The better path is to be a guide; offer the patient a map of the territory and a compass. This is all you can do.

Safeguard Your Heart

Do not offer patients your heart nor over-concern for their welfare. Protect yourself with a barrier lest in their pain they breach your heart.

Patients Are Human, Not Always Kind

Patients are not always good, kind people. They are human, as you are and will fail, as you fail. They will antagonise or speak negatively about you. They are not always honest or nice. You need to understand why.

Finding Professional Support

Find support where you can; trustworthy peers, good training and most of all an experienced supervisor not afraid to tell the truth. These will be rare people.

There Are Many Injustices

Do not believe all is sweetness and light in this field for it is not. It reflects life and life has many injustices. Do not become despondent because the work has its own rewards. Often, it may be the only reward you get.

Patient Sensitivity and Dignity

Patients have human rights; they do not have to give information or fill in your forms. Do not force them to do so.

Eliciting Information Can Be Difficult

Getting information out of someone who does not know you and is afraid of their symptoms [and of you] is not easy. You have to find a balance between getting the information without leaving the patient feeling embarrassed or diminished by the experience. Remember:

- patients give out information in different ways
- diagnoses or assessments can take more than one visit
- information is not given in a linear way
  i.e. you may have a list of questions but the patient will not offer their story in that order. Do not make them repeat because you failed to take adequate notes.

Key Learning 24 The Broad Learning Needed
There is more than diagnosis, treatment or aftercare. You have to be aware of many to offer the best possible care.

It is easy for mental health workers to forget the patient is firstly a fellow human being, with a separate life outside their illness. I can't count the number of times I have heard so-called professionals saying things like;

- ☹ 'I'll just slot you in this appointment..'
- ☹ 'I'll see you on Friday at 2pm..' [no choice given]
- ☹ 'she's a depressive' or 'he's a schizophrenic' [they do have a private life and personality too, outside illness]
- ☹ 'you know what so and so [named patient] did'... [guffaws from colleagues in staff canteen]

If such behaviour is widespread in your environment, it is a toxic workplace and it is better to find another post where patients are respected and where you feel safe to learn.

****

Summary of Key Learning Points:

Key Learning 21 The Continuum Scale
See the diagram above. This demonstrates that mental illness is on a continuum with mental health – we all fit somewhere along this sliding scale, which moves as life events touch us.

Key Learning 22 Humans Crave to be Different!
We hate being isolated through differences, while not wanting to run with the wolf pack!

Key Learning 23 Find Parallel Experiences
See if you can think of any parallel experiences, which will help you understand how the patient might be experiencing life.

Key Learning 24 The Broad Learning Needed
There is more than diagnosis, treatment or aftercare. You have to be aware of many to offer the best possible care.

'Our smallest actions may affect profoundly the whole lives of people who have nothing to do with us'
Somerset Maughan, Virtue

7 Early Signs of Mental Illnesses

Contents of this Chapter:

We are already quite a way into this book and the patient has not yet arrived on the GP's doorstep. We need to consider how they get there.

I would like to set the scene with a brief explanation about mental health and freedom. This part of the chapter refers to patients with enduring mental illness and is not about the mental health act but the reason it exists.

Free to Roam?

Many people outside the field wonder why people with serious mental problems are not in the care of professionals. This sort of thinking happens after a murderous attack or suicide has been reported in the newspapers and there are moral panics about public safety issues.

People in Western society are free to more or less do what they like unless they break a law. No one can be hospitalised or imprisoned 'without just cause' and certainly not because a neighbour thinks them a nuisance or they appear to act strangely.

Our laws both protect and make us vulnerable. There has to be enough evidence to convict a criminal or forcibly hospitalise a dangerous patient without acting indiscrimately on innocent or eccentric persons who are not harming anyone - even if someone is annoyed by their behaviour.

The Crown Prosecution Service decides whether or not to prosecute a potential criminal. The police have to present a good case. They need written evidence such as witness statements, alibis, confessions. Forensic scientists look for physical evidence; DNA, fibres, fingerprints. If there is enough evidence the CPS prosecutes and the criminal is taken to court.

In the case of mental illness, evidence or diagnosis is difficult to obtain because most of it is hidden in the three areas of thinking, feeling and behaviour. A Psychiatrist and his team will have to prove to a Tribunal that the potential patient is seriously ill and a danger to themselves or others or both.

If the Tribunal are in agreement, the ill person will become a voluntary patient or else involuntary patient sectioned under the Mental Health Act. Treatment will follow. Neither the mental health professionals nor the Tribunal will forcibly hospitalise someone if they are not ill enough to warrant this treatment, because they will be breaching human rights.

It is difficult to decide the point at which reasonable behaviour turns into something that requires police intervention. No professional worth their salary will want to have their patient sectioned, because this will seriously affect that patient's future. This is why they err on the side of caution whilst the public see only bizarre behaviour they want out of their street, no matter what the consequences.

Key Learning 25 Free to Roam?
There are ethical, medical and legal reasons why those with serious mental illness are not 'locked away' as some would wish.

Why Mental Illness Can Be Difficult to Spot

The trouble is it is easy to see signs of mental illness when they are full blown, but these may have:

- Taken months or years to manifest
- Had no outward sign – e.g. the suicidal person who has not revealed mental anguish
- Happened away from their usual community - prisoners, travelling businessmen, people in hospital
- happened so quickly everyone is taken by surprise
- the result of an unforeseen catastrophe or life event

Regular Mental Health Service Users

If a patient has a known major mental illness such as schizophrenia the family should have:

- a professional on hand, even if they have to wait for an appointment.
- a comprehensive care plan, compiled during remission, which will outline a structured care programme for dealing with future episodes
- an aftercare programme of support.

These measures are to ensure no patient who needs care slips under the net; yet they continue to do so.

First Episode Patients

For those who are not regular mental health service users, the problems are more difficult from the first stage of awareness through to diagnosis to treatment. Why is this?

There are two periods of time involved in the onset of mental illness. Some take months or years to manifest. Changes can be so subtle that even closest family will not be aware of them until family life starts to break down or a serious incident happens. However, in some cases, the onset is so fast that it knocks everyone for six.

Early Signs of Mental Illness

Early signs of mental illness can be extremely difficult to spot, even for family and professionals.

We all have days when nothing goes right and we get irritable or withdrawn; these are normal reactions to adverse situations. Teenagers are prone to dark moods and changes in character. So how does anyone recognise signs which need attention; stress, early stages of depression or severe mental illness?

It's a bit like detective work; slowly and painstakingly gathering evidence - the general indicators until proper diagnosis is made:

1. change in behaviour not associated with specific events
2. changes for the worse in appearance, hygiene or weight
3. marked change to usual routine
4. changes in mood which are otherwise inexplicable

I will give you a few examples, but perhaps you can add to this list as you come across examples from your own clinical practice or from your own life experience:

Change In Behaviour

- quiet person becomes snappy or aggressive
- confident person becomes withdrawn and tearful
- outgoing person stops socialising
- someone good at their jobs makes a lot of mistakes

Changes in Appearance, Hygiene or Weight

- clean and tidy person becomes dishevelled
- puts on or takes off excessive amount of weight in a short time frame

- gait changes - confident to slouched & lack of eye contact
- clothing suddenly either drab or too colourful or bizarre

Withdrawal or Marked Change to Usual Routine

- increased social activity to excessive level
- furtive instead of open about where they are going
- withdraws or hides from people
- stops enjoying activity

Changes In Mood Which are Otherwise Inexplicable

- quiet person becomes loud and vociferous
- confident person becomes sad or fearful
- calm person is aggressive or excessively anxious

These signs can appear over a considerable period of time; months instead of days. Imagine how stressful this is for relatives let alone the potential patient. How will you best advise relatives? Not easy, but consider the following.

Key Learning 26 Early Warning Signs
Marked changes in behaviour, mood, routine, appearance can signify the potential onset of mental illness.

Dangers of Over Reacting to Symptoms

If a relative over reacts to these signs, most likely they will be rejected and left feeling hurt or mystified. Their loved one might feel misunderstood [if there is a rational cause and they have chosen not to share it, through embarrassment, shame or fear of over burdening relatives].

Rational causes can vary:

- job loss, not revealed to loved ones out of shame
- sexual or intimacy problems
- bullying, structural or management or status changes
- financial problems
- feeling of diminishment – in work, school, profession

- close friend with serious problems
- health issue which they don't want to worry relatives with

If a professional over-reacts, they risk:

- being rejected when the patient really does need help
- being seen by relatives as patronising
- giving the patient a false label of mental illness
- losing the trust of patient and their relatives
- losing credibility and confidence in their expertise

As always, watchful waiting [as the Government calls it] is the key. Relatives might come and see you, perhaps having suffered for months without sharing their fears. Whilst convention says the patient must ask for help, please consider THEY [the relative] are the patient at this moment!

Early Stages

Although you cannot act, you can listen and suggest a plan to worried relatives:

1 look after their own mental health
2 unobtrusively monitor their loved one
3 try to keep life as normal as possible
4 don't give up pleasurable activity, socialising or routines
5 make sure they are supported, by yourself or some other professional, and know where to find this
6 offer an advance appointment, even if months ahead
7 encourage them to keep a progress plan or a personal journal - something which helps them maintain hope
8 watch out for the crisis point and dive into action

Key Learning 27 Learning Not to Over React
It is vital not to make assumptions and over react to potential signs of impending illness.

Action for Relatives

First Stage

Relatives will know the potential patient better than you do. They will want to help [hopefully] and will be able to gauge reaction. They can put themselves as far as possible into their loved one's shoes to ask the rhetorical question 'what do I [patient] want from them [relative]'.

If the person is not willing to talk, perhaps it would be easier indirectly;

- a nice card or letter
- an email
- talking during a walk or outing

All these may open up channels of communication, although nothing is guaranteed. The relative[s] need to put the onus on themselves, avoid blaming and use the term 'I' and not 'you make me..' thus:

- ♥ 'I'm hoping I haven't got this wrong, but I feel ...'
- ♥ 'forgive me if I say this because I am concerned..'
- ♥ 'I am feeling anxious that..'
- ♥ 'I really want to talk about ... because I care for you'

Trust can easily be lost and it is not anyone's business to over-interfere with someone else's life, even a spouse or partner of long standing.

The Crisis Point

Monitor, watch and wait is all anyone can do, until the crisis happens. When it does, the relative or you must dive through this window of opportunity and act.

There will be an event or situation, or moment of realization on someone's behalf, or a time when the family is near breaking point. It may be a breaking of a pent up emotion; something heard, read or seen that triggers reaction; a sudden insight by the loved one that they are not well; a critical act that triggers the need for professional intervention.

Hospitalising Without Sectioning

My personal experience is when a friend had a manic attack and I was called by her worried parents. She was very ill by then, wandering around with matches then lying on the floor talking to her voices.

After a couple of hours listening to her rambling, I managed to plead with her she was not well and please could I take her to hospital. As soon as she said a faint 'yes' I took her to my car immediately without saying anything else. No arguments, forcing or police involved – it was very calm. Half an hour later she was sedated, in bed on a ward.

My point is that this is better than having several burly policemen arrive on a doorstep and manhandle a terrified young lady who is under a delusion they are attacking her.

This is one point of arrival at a centre for treatment. The better one is arrival at a GP surgery, by someone who knows there is something wrong, but can't put a finger on it.

Key Learning 28 Cautions for Carers

Carers and workers need caution when someone is fragile. Time needs to be taken; look for windows of opportunity to allow the patient to decide to be hospitalised.

Reasons for Non-Arrival of Patients

Mental illnesses can be diagnosed only in patients who arrive at a professional organisation or individual therapist for treatment. Some cases do not come to attention of a professional and rarely will because:

- families tolerate odd behaviours
- abusive families create and absorb crises; even experienced Social Workers can be fooled into thinking them 'normal'
- depressive illness can be perceived as sadness or laziness
- mania is tolerated as high jinks by dysfunctional families

- people are often cared for within their own cultures
- illness is unobserved in those who live alone
- family shame prevents disclosure
- suicide figures are hidden because Coroners with insufficient evidence record deaths as by misadventure – sometimes they do this to protect relatives feelings
- some illness spontaneously go into remission

In the case of seriously ill patients unaware of their illness, as in schizophrenia when insight is lost, medication is prescribed but never taken and appointments not kept. Some families collude under the false belief that the problems will go away. Under conflicting demands of human rights versus mental health legislation everyone is in a dilemma. The police cannot arrest and detain a person because someone claims to be afraid of them or a malicious person says something untruthful or someone misreads a situation. Both medical and legal people need to be sure there is a correct solution and a good outcome for all; patient, relatives and the public at large.

Key Learning 29 Reasons for Non Arrival for Treatment
It is vital to look at social and cultural reasons for patients not brought to those who can help. Forced treatment is a last resort.

Moral Panics

Before concluding this chapter, I want to say a few words about mental illness that goes untreated. This hot topic comes up when there has been a horrific murder in the news. There are more murders by so-called sane people than anyone with a psychiatric history but most people refuse to believe this for their own comfort. It is easier to have someone to blame or a rational explanation. No one likes to think a sane person commits murder because it strikes fear into the heart of the community. Then, there is a moral panic about untreated seriously ill people and everyone uses the opportunity to get on their soapbox about the problem and its resolution. Although there are a few dangerous forensic mental disorders, there are very few people relative to the size of population who have these conditions. Bizarre behaviour, of which there is a considerable amount, is not the same as potentially murderous delusions of attack.

Lack of Mental Health Education

The problem really is, the public have never been educated about mental illness. Imagination rather than knowledge is the source of their fear; that and scapegoating as I have already explained. Now that citizenship and health are part of the national curriculum, this problem could have been better addressed in the decades to come. However, it will take longer thanks to the Government encouraging schools to discuss mental health but not insisting upon this as part of the standards. What a waste of a golden opportunity!

Key Learning 30 Moral Panic

Moral panics about mental illness are to do with lack of education and the resulting fear about what dangers exist for the public.

****

Summary of Key Learning Points:

Key Learning 25 Free to Roam?

There are ethical, medical and legal reasons why those with serious mental illness are not 'locked away' as some would wish.

Key Learning 26 Early Warning Signs

Marked changes in behaviour, mood, routine, appearance can signify the potential onset of mental illness.

Key Learning 27 Learning Not to Over React

It is vital not to make assumptions and over react to potential signs of impending illness.

Key Learning 28 Cautions for Carers

Carers and workers need caution when someone is fragile. Time needs to be taken; look for windows of opportunity.

Key Learning 29 Reasons for Non Arrival for Treatment

It is vital to look at social and cultural reasons for patients not brought to those who can help. Forced treatment is a last resort.

Key Learning 30 Moral Panic

Moral panics about mental illness are to do with lack of education and the resulting fear about what dangers exist for the public.

MAJOR MENTAL ILLNESSES: MEDICAL DIAGNOSES & TREATMENTS

'Possibly Davis, like many investigators, was disposed to find what he looked for' H G Wells, Star Begotten

8 Medical Diagnoses

Contents of this Chapter:

In this chapter, I am going to cover the topic of diagnosis – both why it is necessary and the process.

Terminology: Diagnosis v Assessment

Diagnosis is a medical term, Greek in origin, and means to distinguish. According to my dictionary, it is described as 'identification of disease by investigation of symptoms and history'. Diagnosis is strictly a medical term although many alternative practitioners use the term too. Other therapists prefer to use the term assessment which is gentler and does not smack of medical matters.

Those who practice complementary medicine do not always accept medical diagnoses or treat on the basis of such diagnoses - so interpretations will be different. For example

- a doctor might diagnose and treat phobia
- an alternative practitioner might see the same problem as psycho-social, spiritual or a symbolic form of distress.

As an example, one of my early blunders when I practiced as a hypnotherapist was in treating a man who came to me because he had lost his precious watch. I thought his issue was to do with time and disappointment. It was far too many sessions before I learned that he had recently been bereaved of his wife. His symbolic search was for relief from this bereavement, not the watch nor the time it seemed to signify.

Key Learning 31 Diagnosis is a Medical Term
Many alternative practitioners do not use diagnoses in the medical sense; they prefer a holistic approach; mind, body, spirit.

What Diagnosis Is For

In diagnosing, a doctor is:

- ∇ trying to understand the origin of the illness
- ∇ taking note of the symptoms
- ∇ offering treatment to alleviate symptoms
- ∇ planning aftercare to prevent relapse

In the first book of this series I used the analogy of decorating a room to explain diagnosis. There are certain steps involved in both:

- ∇ awareness something is wrong
- ∇ sizing up the situation
- ∇ make a list of what needs doing
- ∇ make a plan of the resources you need
- ∇ make sure the resources are available
- ∇ carry out the plan
- ∇ check and make sure all is ok

In decorating a room without such a plan you might do the jobs in the wrong order, order the wrong number of rolls of wallpaper, select colours that do not go together and end up unhappy, having spent a lot of money.

Incorrect diagnosis is far more serious and can lead to the wrong treatment, distressed patient, angry relatives and embarrassed professionals. There is no guarantee that correct diagnosis will end in a successful outcome, but at least there will be a fighting chance of success.

Key Learning 32 Diagnosis or Assessment
Both these terms are used for the process of analysis which forms the backbone of future treatment plans.

Steps For a Typical Medical Diagnosis

Case History

A case history enables the patient to tell their story. This does not always happen within one session as it does in Primary Care, but may take several appointments. The professional is looking for:

1. the chain of events which lead to the illness
2. if they have had similar reactions before
3. family health history, both physical and mental
4. changes in mood and /or behaviour
5. how they are feeling now

These questions will enable the professional to establish:

1. where the problems might have started
2. how well the patient is able to deal with life
3. if there is a history of similar illness in the family
4. how long the illness has been affecting the patient
5. how serious the current problem is

Mental & Physical Examination

The patient might be asked to complete certain psychological tests [Becks Depression Inventory for example] to determine their mental state. There will be a physical examination which will help determine the type of illness and its severity. For example a blood test might indicate high levels of lithium in the blood which may indicate mania.

Application of the Diagnosis

Once examinations are complete, the Psychiatrist is ready to apply knowledge using DSMIV [or a similar manual] and make an initial diagnosis. This diagnosis will change as further evidence comes to light. Doctors count on their experience, for example how cultural or ethnic considerations may affect the diagnosis or treatment plan.

The Diagnostic Manual [DSMIV]

Psychiatrists use a version of 'The Diagnostic and Statistics Manual'(DSM). This manual is a publication produced by the American Psychiatric Association and is used world-wide to aid diagnoses.

DSMIV contains lists of criteria (conditions) for mental conditions which are currently considered mental illnesses. As a piece of social history, it is interesting to note that homosexuality used to appear as a mental condition but no longer does so.

DSM IV contains a list of symptoms for each disorder and a range of severity. The guidelines are based on observation and research. Each condition has a set of numbers and letters called keys which allow the practitioner to gauge the severity of the condition.

Although this manual is useful, Psychiatrists have to consider what they know about patient's backgrounds, for example their cultural background and beliefs. Mental illness cannot be divorced from its community setting and it is vital that many facets of the patient's life form a part of the considerations for diagnosis.

MIMS

Have you ever wondered how GP's know which of the many pharmaceutical preparations to prescribe? They use a manual which describes not only chemical content but also contra-indications, dosage and cost of all the drugs currently on the UK market.

Mims is 'the most up-to-date prescribing information for doctors and pharmacists' as the publishers describe it. Haymarket Medical is a specialist publisher for the medical field. Mims is a quarterly booklet which contains all the information doctors need to allow them to make clinical decisions. MIMS is now available on-line.

All drugs have to be approved [a process I described in **Understanding Mental Illness**] not only through drug trials but also a legal license issued by the Department of Health.

Key Learning 33 Stages of Diagnosis
These follow a logical order; case history, mental & physical examination, diagnosis [using DSMIV], application of analysis, treatment, aftercare.

Cultural Factors and Diagnosis

Some cultures are tolerant and encourage factors which in Western culture could be mis-interpreted as hallucinations or delusions:

- voodoo and witchcraft cultures
- religious ecstasies, spiritual images or speaking in tongues
- ancestor worship where it is accepted that ancestors appear to the living to advise them
- spiritualists who communicate with the dead

A psychiatrist has to take these factors into account when trying to diagnose schizophrenia for example, as it is a hugely stigmatised disorder.

****

Summary of Key Learning Points:

Key Learning 31 Diagnosis is a Medical Term
Many alternative practitioners do not use diagnoses in the medical sense; they prefer a holistic approach; mind, body, spirit.

Key Learning 32 Diagnosis or Assessment
Both of these terms are used for the process of analysis which forms the backbone of future treatment plans.

Key Learning 33 Stages of Diagnosis
These follow a logical order; case history, mental & physical examination, diagnosis [using DSMIV], application of analysis [& doctor's experience] treatment

'It is only .. Darknesse that can give Perspective to our Fabrick, for there is no Light without Darknesse and no Substance without Shadowe' Peter Ackroyd, Hawksmoor

9 The Major Mental Illnesses

Contents of this Chapter:

So, now we are ready to look at some of these individual mental health conditions, or mental illnesses, in detail. Remember, these are medical diagnoses. If you go to a complementary or alternative practitioner, they might offer a different explanation for symptoms, which is why I have separated these chapters.

Suggested Diagnostic Exercise:

Remember the vignettes you read earlier? I have tried to provide one vignette for each of the following diagnoses.

It might be an interesting exercise to read through the following sets of symptoms - see if you can apply them to one of the vignettes I described in Chapter 4.

1. read the symptoms for one of the mental illnesses
2. go back and read each vignette [see chapter 4] in turn
3. decide if any of the symptoms apply

4. make your own notes
5. start again at 1 and work your way through again

If you don't want to do this exercise I have put suggested answers at the end of this chapter.

****

Brief Psychotic Disorder

Symptoms:

- Hallucinations – visual / auditory
- Delusions – powerful beliefs not based on reality
- Withdrawal and isolation
- Dishevelled appearance
- Inability to care for the self

Brief Psychotic Disorder is the medical term for what many lay people term nervous breakdown. It is not a breakdown of the nervous system but hyper-activation of brain chemistry, which results in extreme [heightened] sensitivity.

During psychosis, perception recedes under delusions and hallucinations. Life becomes highly disorganised because real world cannot be separated from the delusional one; in other words, the sufferer loses the insight that they are ill and what is happening is not real.

Closest to the experiences of psychoses are nightmares. Imagine waking from a nightmare to find you are still in it; that person or thing is still chasing you. Imagine the horror, were you to wake up and find your partner or spouse lying dead next to you - you had killed them under a delusion they were attacking you. Next time you hear about a mentally ill killer, remember this scenario.

The most vivid depictions of psychosis that I have seen are in these movies:

A Beautiful Mind - which depicts the life of mathematician John Nash. I recommend this movie to all students of mental health. Nash was an exceptional person and managed to cope with life-long schizophrenia by using his gift of analysis. Nash realizes his human hallucinations are never growing older, as his own family and friends age. It is enough for him to retain a precarious grip on reality.

The Matrix – a science fantasy where Neo ['The One'] has to get inside a computer game in order to free mankind from the virtual reality matrix into which robots have entrapped them. Neo experiences the blur as he moves inside and outside both worlds, not knowing which is real and which is not – perhaps both are not.

Of all mental symptoms, psychosis is the most terrifying and the most damaging. Some people do not recover. In the case of schizophrenia, psychoses can be controlled by drugs but there is no cure.

If you consider the experience of delusions, visual and auditory hallucinations, physical symptoms become clearer;

- disorganised speech
- withdrawal from the real world
- dishevelled appearance

These increase as the patient retreats into this twilight world. Imagine the fear, isolation and loneliness; what it must be like, for a loved one to experience their partner or friend in this state.

It is no wonder that carers of patients with such illnesses are in grave danger of becoming mentally ill themselves, which is why carers are now entitled to regular mental assessments.

Key Learning 34 Parallel Experience and Psychoses
If you have not experienced the symptoms of psychosis, it is easier if you consider parallel experiences OR read a book or watch a movie which draws the real life experience in fictional form.

****

Depressive Illness

Basic Symptoms:

- ➢ Extreme low mood, which persists
- ➢ Lack of energy and sleep disturbance

- Withdrawal and isolation
- Lack of concentration and inability for self care
- Feelings of worthlessness or guilt
- Persistent thoughts of death / actively suicidal
- Persisting pains - headache ['tight band' across the brow] or other medically unexplained pain

The difference between sadness and depression is like the difference between a cold and pneumonia. People who have not experienced depression find it hard to imagine because they associate it with feeling depressed or having the blues, which describe ordinary life sadness.

The nearest associated life experiences are bereavement and rejection in love which share the features of pain, isolation and sense of unreality.

Depressive illness manifests as extreme exhaustion, a feeling of utter hopelessness, worthlessness of the self and enduring isolation. This is difficult for family and friends to deal with and many withdraw leaving the depressed person feeling isolated and guilty. There is often associated physical pain which is unexplained by any physical cause.

Suicidal Urges

Severe depressive illness can be lethal as people of all ages and backgrounds take their own lives. Suicidal urges are symptoms of severe depression as are hallucinations and delusions.

Sometimes it is only a patient's lack of energy which prevents suicidal urges turning into the act of suicide. The danger time comes as energy levels rise; this is the time for vigilance.

Depression can lift spontaneously or persist for months or years. Recovery is erratic and slow and there may be recurrent episodes. There is no cure as such but the patient can learn to control the illness and to recognise the signs of impending illness so that they can seek early help.

Key Learning 35 Depression and Isolation
The overwhelming experience in depression is that of existential loneliness; a deep sense of worthlessness, hopelessness and isolation.

****

Figure 9 The Experience of Psychosis

Eating Disorders

Basic Symptoms:

- Self-induced recurrent vomiting or purging
- Restricting intake of food
- Obsessed with body weight or food
- Variable extreme moods
- Tooth decay, menstrual cycles disrupted
- Belief in being judged by appearance

Do you remember thinking you were fat as a teenager and when you were older you looked at your photos and realized you were a normal size? It's the same sort of mental trick in the minds of people with eating disorders. It is difficult for families to understand when their loved one weighs less than 6 stones and still believes they are fat. These eating disorders used to manifest mainly in girls but boys are rapidly catching up.

Anorexia means restricting intake of food whereas bulimia is binge-eating followed by purging (laxatives or self-induced vomiting). There are some aspects of both in eating disorders so doctors no longer separate anorexia from bulimia.

Patients are both obsessed food and crave it, however, the drive not to eat or to purge are impossible to control and often frighten them. Eating-disordered patients do not receive the sympathetic approach they need in hospital because nurses misunderstand the illness and belief it is self-induced; a similar negative attitude shown to suicidal patients who end up in Accident and Emergency departments.

Force-feeding does not work long-term as patients do not learn to address food obsession. Nagging does not help. Many patients fear their lack of control around food and want to be cured but are unable to do this alone. Clinicians find it hard to treat these patients knowing a large proportion of those admitted to hospital will die of multiple organ failure.

There is a new community treatment, which is gaining popularity, in which a small group of patients live together in a special hostel whilst being treated on a more informal basis.

It is very difficult to get people with eating disorders to talk about food. If clinicians do this clumsily, they are liable to have their patients walk out. It is useful to use indirect and gentle means such as physical observation, waiting for the patient to talk first, or asking the patient why they think their parent/teacher/friend is worried about them. Sometimes the subject of food is best avoided altogether in the early stages, in favour of discussions about other perceived problem areas.

Key Learning 36 Eating Disorders & Their Treatment
Eating problems are very difficult to treat and require long term input. Some say they are to do with control and avoidance.

****

Mania

Basic Symptoms:

- Increase in energy [psychomotor agitation]
- Very talkative with rapid speech– excessively so.
- Decreased need for sleep
- Patient has an inflated opinion of their abilities
- Rapid swings of mood

Mania rarely manifests alone, although I did meet one patient with this phenomena many years ago. It is the high mood of a patient with manic-depressive psychosis [MDP]; mania and depression being at either end of the mood scale. This disorder has been given many names over the years, including bi-polar disorder, manic depression and MDP or manic-depressive psychosis.

In my book **Understanding Mental Illness**, I recommended a book for trainees on MDP which I would like to repeat.

Jackie Lyden, a Journalist, wrote a biographical account of her mother's illness in **Daughter of the Queen of Sheba**. There are many books about mania and MDP but I found this particularly poignant as it contains a day-to-day life account of this terrible illness and the trail of destruction to family life. You may find it sobering that 20% of such patients commit suicide in despair; an indication of their suffering.

Mania is expressed in bouts of frenzied activity and thinking. The patient is frightened about this lack of control. What it is <u>not</u> is extreme happiness. Laughing in a mirthless kind of way, is the laughter of mania.

Patients in a manic state may overspend, indulge in prolific sexual activity [and later be bitterly ashamed of it], carry out dangerous activities, act irresponsibly or irrationally to the detriment of their own and their family's lives. Their thoughts are irrational and inflated, with an inflated belief in themselves and their ideas.

Mania cannot be controlled. The brain chemistry is over-exited and only medication controls it. This is one of the few mental illnesses for which medical treatment is pre-requisite [the others being psychoses, schizophrenia and depression of suicidal intensity].

Lithium is not pleasant and after several years leads to a kind of Parkinsonism [shaking] of hands or kidney problems. It is difficult for patients with mania to maintain a medication regime for many reasons:

- the bad side effects
- psychological impact - knowing you must take a drug or cocktail of drugs every day for the rest of your life.
- lack of insight when ill; they do not accept they are ill
- the buzz of a high can be a powerful drug in itself

Key Learning 37 Mania is Not Happiness
Mania is nothing like happiness, joy or glee. It is uncomfortable, frightening, uncontrollable.

****

Obsessive Compulsive Disorder (OCD)

Everyone will have experienced a mild form of **compulsion** [or urge]. These are examples of urges:

- eat or drink, even when not hungry or thirsty
- to go and do another activity
- to leave a situation because it is uncomfortable
- to make a comment, even if inappropriate

Everyone will have experienced a need to **check** something, because they are unsure. These are examples of checking:

- that you have locked the front door [before going out]
- you have locked your car or bike
- you have switched off a gas or electric point
- you think you have forgotten something
- looking to the right and left before crossing a road

Everyone has **rituals** to get them through daily life. These are examples of rituals:

- carrying luck charms
- actions before an event to ensure success
- religious practices or services
- football chants
- using specific numbers for the national lottery

These behaviours or rituals of checking and compulsion are quite normal in most contexts and are there to protect us. Imagine:

- ➢ if you did not check the road was clear, before stepping out – wham! Instant death.
- ➢ If you did not check the gas or electric was off – come back from your shopping to find no house and the fire brigade hosing down the remains
- ➢ If you did not check the door was locked, come back to find your possessions rifled, filth over your property [burglars

sometimes defecate on property, as a sign of their perceived power]

Obsessive compulsive disorder [OCD] is comprised of all these elements but to an excess we call obsessive. Checking becomes pathological when it interferes and takes over everyday life.

A common type of OCD is cleaning. Cleaning is a normal part of everyday life, but when someone cleans for hours on end, scrubbing their hands raw and starting again if they miss something out, this is pathological. We can then say, that the cleaning has become not an object of cleansing, but a ritual designed to ward something off – usually an unpleasant set of thoughts or a feared event.

At this point, the cleaning ceases to make sense even to the person cleaning, but they are unable to stop– it has become a compulsion and a ritual. There are persistent ideas, thoughts or images and these can only be allayed by the rituals the patient has set for him or herself.

I have set the above information out in a more stylized way below so that you can see clearly how obsessions [mental] are related to compulsions [physical – i.e. the rituals].

Mental aspects – Obsessions

- 1: persistent idea – the house is contaminated
- 2: persistent thought – burglary of their home
- 3: persistent image – thinking about crude sexual acts

Physical aspects – Compulsions

The examples below refer to the respective numbered examples above:

- compulsive ritual for 1: constant hand washing
- compulsive ritual for 2: checking & testing of locks
  compulsive ritual for 3: praying to negate guilt

OCD is not a common illness and occurs in 1.5 to 2% of the population in a year. There are elements of OCD within the disorder known as psychosis where the patient wards off the terrors of hallucinations and delusions with rituals. In the medical model, OCD is thought to be caused by chemical disturbances in the brain.

Medical Treatments
Medical treatment of choice is anti psychotic medication.

Key Learning 38 Tri Part Symptoms of OCD
Obsession, compulsion, ritual all play a part in OCD.

****

Phobia
Phobia is from a Greek word meaning a fear or dread. We all fear something, whether or not that fear is rational. Irrational fear is at the terror end of the scale of anxiety.

Fear is normal and has ensured man's survival. If early men had not feared lions they would have been wiped out, because they would not have run away from them. In Australia, if people did not fear spiders and avoid them, there would be more deaths from poisonous spiders like the black widow.

These are everyday fears:

- being out in the dark
- fear of failing
- fear of certain insects or animals
- fear of feelings like love

Phobias start as mild anxieties which multiply and spread out to areas outside the initial fear. For example mild anxiety around spiders can increase over time to phobic level, when a patient sees a drawing or crack in a pavement that resembles a spider and becomes fearful. As normal anxiety increases its intensity to dread, then it becomes pathological.

Common types of Phobias are:

- agora – fear of open spaces
- arachna – fear of spiders
- blood/infection – fear of being contaminated
- claustro – fear of being in a confined space
- situational – fear of specific situations e.g. flying

Symptoms of Phobia

To be diagnosed as a phobia, a condition must have lasted at least six months. The physical symptoms are the result of the hormone adrenaline which floods the body when the brain senses danger.

Adrenaline causes many symptoms; dizziness, crushing headache, butterfly stomach, tingling, dry mouth, loosening of bowels, fast beating heart, unable to think clearly [we become frozen, like a rabbit in car headlamps].

The mental symptoms include:

- excessive unreasonable fear
- avoidance of the fear

Phobias could have many causes, from negative encounters with the feared object in the past, to reactions to loss.

Phobias are not usually treated with medication unless they are extreme in which case benzodiazepines or beta blockers can reduce the symptoms of anxiety.

The scale on the next page demonstrates the continuum of normal to pathological scale of fear. Fear which tends to reach past the cut off point of normality [shown in this illustration by a vertical line] is considered phobic [pathological] and needs treatment.

Figure 10 Phobia

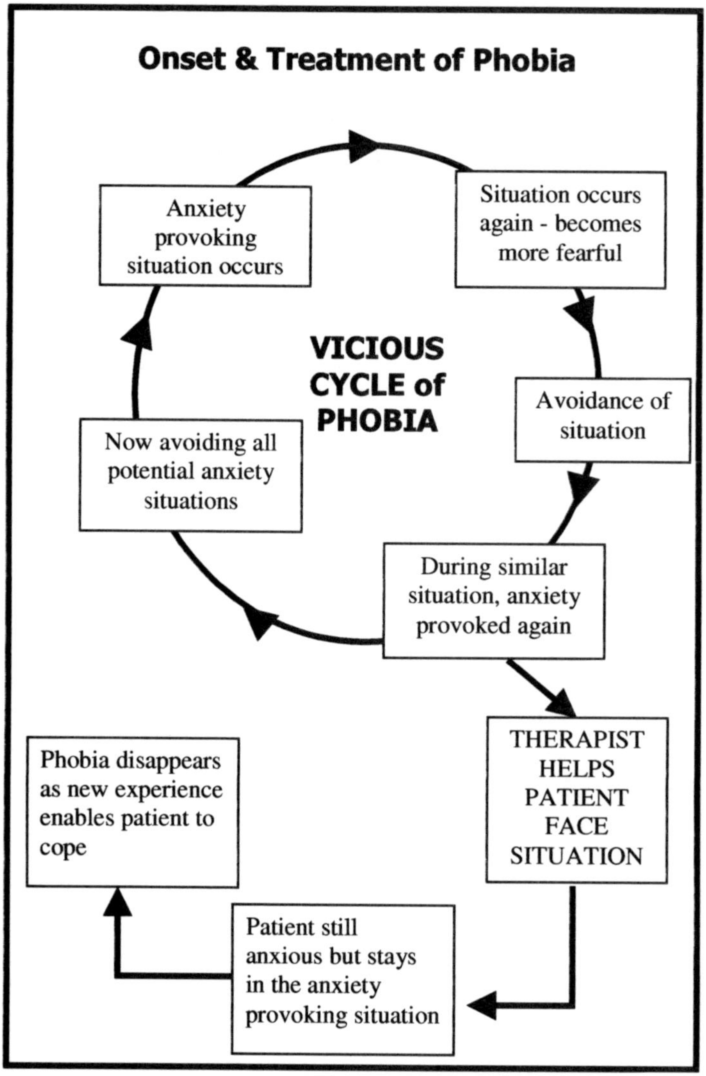

Schizophrenia

Schizophrenia is not easily diagnosed and some clinicians do not accept it as a distinct condition. It has an odd cluster of symptoms that are not easily defined but understandable, I think, in terms of all or some of the following:

- Fragmentation or disorganised thinking processes
- Marked alterations to usual personality
- Disturbances to hearing and vision – auditory and visual hallucinations
- Disturbances of thinking and speech [word salad]
- Loss to the normal sense of sensory input [due to above]
- Loss of social status and self esteem
- Gradual shunning of society – community or friendships
- Marked sense of isolation
- Grief or depression
- Loss of sense of self as a whole person
- Loss of perception of others in the same way [as above]

Schizophrenia is nothing to do with split personality as is commonly thought, however personality can be destroyed because of overwhelming and ongoing symptoms.

The overarching symptoms are loss of touch with the everyday world, a fragmented sense of self-existence and inappropriate emotions which lead to isolation of the patient.

It is truly the most tragic of all the mental illnesses. It is incurable although symptoms can be reduced thanks to the latest anti psychotic medications, which enable many former patients to live in the community.

The patient is unable to distinguish between what is really happening and what is imaginary because the hallucinations are so overwhelming they take over the entire sensory input.

None of us can cope with massive sensory input. Many patients with schizophrenia commit suicide which it is understandable, given the scale of the sensory delusions and overwhelming sense of isolation.

Key Learning 39 Sensory Input
None of us can cope with excessive sensory input; the brain naturally filters excess input out, except in mental illness.

Difficulty in Explaining the Experience of Schizophrenia

It is difficult to describe schizophrenia to someone who has never experienced either the illness or the major symptoms. Reading a list of symptoms does not give anything like an idea of how devastating an illness it is and how heroic the patients are, that manage to survive.

I am lucky in having experienced psychosis on two occasions in my life, therefore I can find some parallel experiences to explain how marked sensory perception changes your outlook on the real world, your feelings about others, your basic trust.

Schizophrenia is more cruel than any illness – it affects every area of what make us human; reason, trust, insight, clarity of purpose, emotions, analysis, a sense of continuity through daily life experiences and peace of mind.

Time has no real meaning and there is no sense to the experiences of schizophrenia; the very things that ground us in sanity – 'I am here today and doing this, tomorrow I will go here or there, this is how I will resolve that'.

Imagine your whole world turned upside down; you don't know if it is dawn or dusk. I can remember this period of my life quite well when I was psychotic, looking out of the window and trying to figure out which end of the day it was. It is a very disorientating experience.

If you want to see how the bizarre world of madness can be used to create great art, look at the art of Dutch painter Hieronymus Bosch, Edvard Munch, Francisco Goya, Salvador Dali, Vincent Van Gogh, Richard Dadd, Walter Sickert [suspected as being Jack the Ripper].

As psychosis develops, you lose trust with loved ones – and they become terrified by you. There is no such resolution and no continuity for these sad patients.

The sense of isolation is overwhelming, because no one shares your experience. There is no awakening until antipsychotics reduce the worst symptoms - by which time you may have lost everything you cared about.

1 Imax Cinema

The way I explained delusions and hallucinations in my last book was to refer to them in terms of an Imax 3D movie. By the way, most people call these films but I use the American term. To me, film is what you put in the camera; a movie is the correct term for the product.

A brief warning about Imax. Some of you might not be able to cope with the sensory experience of 3D. The experience is super-real 3D and if you have any kind of epilepsy or sensory disturbance you should see your GP for advice before attending a screening.

Imax screens are huge, around 21 metres wide by 15 metres tall (6 double decker buses) with as many as 40 speakers. The curved screen and sound system are designed to surround the audience with sound and action such that you experience virtual reality – a 3D sense of being inside the movie. Those who regularly play 3D computer games may have some idea of what it is like.

During a movie, if the person sitting next to you spoke, you would be unlikely to make out what they were saying because your focus is totally on the visual and auditory input from the movie.

Imagine you are not going to see a time limited movie, but that this is happening around you every day. And it is not a nice travelogue or space travel you are taking part in but a terrifying nightmare.

It is a much enhanced type of the sensory trick we experience when watching ordinary movies; daily life is suspended as we get into the story and start to empathise and believe in 'the characters in the movie. Only patients are unable to leave after the movie is finished, because it does not finish – it happens around them and becomes blurred with reality.

For those of you who are interested. there are Imax cinemas in the following major cities:

Belfast	Glasgow	Manchester
Birmingham	London SE1	
Bradford	London SW7	

Key Learning 40 Imax and 3D Experience
Imax cinema is a good way of experiencing virtual reality – a world which does not exist, but you come to believe does, because you are part of the action. This is a way of considering how psychotic experiences affect reality.

2 Movie – 'A Beautiful Mind'

My second example is a movie you can watch. It is called 'A Beautiful Mind' and is the fictionalised biography of Dr John Nash, Nobel prize-winning mathematician.

Nash contacted schizophrenia whilst he was at University. During his time there he was experiencing two separate delusional worlds; espionage and an extraordinary friendship with two hallucinatory characters, one of whom he imagined he was sharing a room with.

Astonishingly, and rarely, Nash was able to gain insight into his delusional world. He used his considerable intellect to challenge what he was experiencing, realizing his hallucinatory friends and enemies were not getting older as he and his real family aged.

Nash is a remarkable man. He not only won a Nobel prize for his work but managed to marry, have a child and carve out a life based on continuing daily attendance at his University, which gave him stability, status and a reason for living.

I can thoroughly recommend this movie. The moviemakers have cleverly merged the delusional and real life experiences of Nash to show the audience how difficult it is to separate the two, even for viewers.

Key Learning 41 A Movie Which Depicts Schizophrenia
'A Beautiful Mind' is an excellent movie which brilliantly depicts the effects of schizophrenia.

3 Experiencing the Dead - in Bereavement

My third example comes from the common experience of bereaved people apparently seeing their loved one in the flesh after death. The person does not appear as a ghost or shadow but 3D as in life. In some cases, just their voice is heard but again as if in real life and talking about present experience, as if the person is still living.

These can be a very distressing experience, for those who are not expecting it and have no religious beliefs to bolster them. If you had asked any of these people if they thought such a thing possible, before being bereaved, then I doubt many would agree. However, it is a well-recorded phenomenon.

This is the manner in which some patients with schizophrenia see their delusional figures. Some see more fragmented version, as their sensory perceptions become confused and shattered by their extreme sensory experiences.

Key Learning 42 Life Experience of Visual Hallucinations
Bereavement is one case where the depth of anguish can trigger hallucinations of seeing the deceased loved one.

Delusions

I wanted to explain, before describing the other symptoms of schizophrenia, about how hallucinations [visual and auditory] and delusions are related.

The patient cannot distinguish, except where medication reduces symptoms, between the real and delusional worlds. Because the mind is geared to reason in humans, the patient tries to connect the disconnected hallucinations with a plausible explanation or real life story – this becomes what medical people call the delusional world of the patient.

Fiction authors regularly create delusional worlds but they are able to separate their life from their created world. Similarly with computer programmers who create 3D games and those who play them.

There is a fine line between reality and delusion which is fuzzy at times. Do you recall being drunk, under the influence of drugs, ill with a fever, highly stressed – that perhaps what you tended to belief about people was different to your normal perception [and even the embarrassment of 'awakening' when you realized your errors]?

Delusions are what really sends someone mad. How can you cope, when the very foundations of your reality [reason] are suddenly pulled away from you.

Fragmentation of Personality

Imagine for a moment life was like this all the time.

Psychiatrists describe fragmentation of the personality to be one of the traits of schizophrenia. I wonder if there is another way of looking at what are seen as individual symptoms? Perhaps the other symptoms follow on from long-term exposure to hallucinations and delusions.

Should it not be surprising that someone is unable to function as a person when their reason is unable to function due to overexposure of sensory stimuli. That in turns leads to lack of self- care, isolation, spiralling down in social terms, job loss.

- How many days could you survive such an experience?
- Can you understand why many people who have schizophrenia commit suicide?
- Do you understand why someone might come to believe they are being attacked and gets a knife out to defend themselves? They are unaware of the reality –an innocent onlooker happens to be standing nearby and is mistaken for one of the characters who is attacking, merely by looking in the wrong direction at the wrong time
- Can you see why patients are deserted; by friends and family who cannot cope with this behaviour?

- Finally, do you understand why patients find it impossible to work, lose their jobs and status and end up homeless?

Next time you see a homeless person, who is dishevelled, wild eyed, drunk or appears drugged, consider – are they not just drunk or beggars but mentally ill people who are ignored by society, out of fear, misunderstanding or perhaps plain lack of care about the situation.

Thought Disorder and 'Word salad'

Patients are unable to think clearly during episodes and may manifest word salad; a meaningless jumble of words, which they believe are making sense. Stroke patients sometimes have this experience also.

This seems to be an indication that the brain wiring has somehow become crossed and distorted, rather like that white noise you hear when radio stations are not quite in tune. Just another of schizophrenia's vile tricks.

Key Learning 43 The Isolating Effect

Delusions, a sense of not being able to communicate with the world, of feeling threatened and not knowing what is going to happen next. This is why schizophrenia is the most feared experience of major mental illness.

Types of Schizophrenia

There are differences in professional views as to the different types of schizophrenia and so DSMIV is under review in this area. However, I will describe the two main forms, both of which I have come across during my career as a mental health worker.

Catatonic Schizophrenia

Now rare, catatonia stupefies the individual who sits in a semi-permanent comatose state. I remember one patient who would sit in the same chair year after year, hardly moving during the day, eating meals but never speaking. A student nurse made considerable efforts to talk to her about the past and the woman started to respond only to sink back when this nurse left for another job and she was again left to her own devices on the ward.

There were many stupefied patients sitting in hopeless silence and isolation until the advent of medication, such as L-Dopa, the synthesised form of dopamine which made such a difference to their lives. Watch the movie **Awakenings** if you can, the moving story of a group of long-term mental patients.

Paranoid Schizophrenia

This type of schizophrenia is distinguished by a specific paranoid delusion. People with this form of the illness can be dangerous if their voices are threatening e.g. directing them to kill. However shocking the acts committed as a result one has to remember this is an illness. Very few patients with this form of the illness are likely to commit murder but some do, which sets off the usual moral panic about all mental patients.

Confusion with Psychopathic Personality Disorder

There is an often publicly misperceived difference between schizophrenia and psychopathic personality disorder.

- A psychopathic person is born with no sense of conscience (morals); they are mentally incapable of distinguishing between right and wrong [morals] because this part of their brain is damaged.
- People with schizophrenia **do** make moral distinctions but act because they are under the influence of delusions.

Causes

No one knows the cause of schizophrenia although work is being carried out on a defective gene thought to create the symptoms. There may be a combination of factors:

- current work at the University of Edinburgh is focusing on the genes DISC1 & PDE4B

- family history of the illness
- breakdown due to prolonged and extreme stress
- drug-induced schizophrenic-like symptoms

About 1% of the population is affected. Usually signs are seen during adolescence but rarely is onset in middle age.

****

Model Answers for the Diagnostic Exercise

And now what you have been waiting for! These are my suggested diagnoses using a medical model, for the vignettes I gave you in Chapter 4.

There is no guarantee the patient will agree to the treatment [for example, taking anti depressants for depressive illness] or to the diagnosis. Only patients sectioned under the current Mental Health Act 1983 can be forcibly detained in hospital for treatment.

Now, how many did you guess? Don't worry if you didn't get them all because, as I said, this is just an exercise to give you an idea of the procedure.

Figure 11 Answers to the Diagnostic Exercise

Name	Diagnosis
Emma	Brief psychosis
Alicia	Depression
Joseph	Eating disorder
Thelma	Mania
Lesley	Obsessive compulsive disorder [OCD]
Alan	Phobia
Sandy	Schizophrenia
Soraya	Normal

Were you surprised about Soraya? Perhaps you thought, as did her colleagues, that she was showing some of the signs of a mental health problem. But, consider her culture. Soraya is culturally torn between that of her parents and the Western culture in which she has been brought up.

Her parents have allowed her a great deal of freedom, but in my vignette Soraya also has anxieties and these are to do with her cultural heritage. She is a shy girl, a bit of a loner and I have tried to portray her as the sort of girl who will not want to make waves with her parents. Her anxiety is about the boy she has met in the restaurant where she eats, and with whom she has fallen in love. Hence, all those takeaways.

Her anxieties increase as time goes on, producing the apparent symptoms of a mental illness.

Let us imagine that there is a good outcome for all and her symptoms reduce; she has good support from her colleagues and is loved by her family so the prognosis is potentially good, as long as she can square things with her family.

Now, if our budding Psychiatrist had questioned her, and was too quick to make a diagnosis{of what??} then Soraya might have had a different outcome.

I hope you can see some of the potential consequences by considering the important questions raised by this vignette.

****

Solitude

Solitude is a state a lot of people wish for until they get it. There are negative and positive things about all states of being.

When people select solitude as a lifestyle they risk being ostracised - as being odd or eccentric. As in Soraya's case, those who choose this lifestyle deliberately can live just as fulfilled a life as the party animal. It does not mean the solitary life is alien nor pathological, although some people seem to find it threatening and would class it as such.

People have many reasons, both positive and negative for choosing a solitary lifestyle; perhaps they

- prefer their own company
- enjoy pursuits that need reflection

- learn best through quiet study
- find creativity in the peace of aloneness
- find social situations uncomfortable or distracting
- have been abused or bullied
- cannot cope with sensory distractions [autism] e.g. noise, light or colour

Equally, there are both valid and pathological reasons for seeking company; perhaps these people:

- enjoy the challenge of being in company
- learn through being with other people
- find creativity through bouncing ideas off others
- feel afraid if they are alone
- are scared of being seen as isolated
- cannot cope with thoughts and feelings when alone

Consider the solitary lifestyle of artists, writers, composers, philosophers, academics or monks and nuns. Is it a sign of pathology if such people use isolation in pursuit of their art or spirituality? I think not.

To end this chapter, I would like you to consider a brief quotation from Anthony Storr's book 'Solitude'.

> 'Perhaps the ability to distance oneself from over-involvement with others and the capacity to make a coherent pattern of one's life are important in attaining peace of mind and mental health.'

****

Summary of Key Learning Points:

Key Learning 34 Parallel Experience and Psychoses
If you have not experienced the symptoms of psychosis, it is easier if you consider parallel experiences OR read a book or watch a movie which draws the real life experience in fictional form.

Key Learning 35 Depression and Isolation

The overwhelming experience in depression is existential loneliness – a sense of worthlessness and isolation.

Key Learning 36 Eating Disorders & Their Treatment

Eating problems are very difficult to treat and require long-term input. Some say they are to do with control and avoidance.

Key Learning 37 Mania is Not Happiness

Mania is nothing like happiness, joy or glee. It is uncomfortable, frightening, uncontrollable.

Key Learning 38 Tri Part Symptoms of OCD

Obsession, compulsion, ritual all play a part in OCD.

Key Learning 39 Sensory Input

None of us can cope with excessive sensory input; the brain naturally filters excess input out, except in mental illness.

Key Learning 40 Imax and 3D Experience

Imax cinema is a good way of experiencing virtual reality – a world which does not exist, but you come to believe does, because you are part of the action. This is a way of considering how psychotic experiences affect reality.

Key Learning 41 A Movie Which Depicts Schizophrenia

'A Beautiful Mind' is an excellent movie which brilliantly depicts the effects of schizophrenia.

Key Learning 42 Life Experience of Visual Hallucinations

Bereavement is one case where the depth of anguish can trigger hallucinations of seeing the deceased loved one.

Key Learning 43 The Isolating Effect

Delusions, a sense of not being able to communicate with the world, of feeling threatened and not knowing what is going to happen next. This is why schizophrenia is the most feared experience of major mental illness.

Figure 12 Overview: Types of Treatment

TYPES OF TREATMENT

MEDICAL

Invasive treatments which include Electro Convulsive therapies and Brain surgery

ALTERNATIVE COMPLEMENTARY THERAPIES

Physical therapies, mind, body, and spirit, Self help, green or eco therapies, art therapies.

TRADITIONAL NON MEDICAL

Psychotherapy, analytical, psychology, Therapeutic community

NON MEDICAL & ALTERNATIVE VIEWS

'the new can be heard only when the old tape becomes completely silent without any effort' Krishnamurti

10 Mainstream Non-Medical Treatments

Contents of this Chapter:

I have included talking therapies and psychological treatments in this section. Although some people would class these with the medical treatments, I have not done so as they do not include invasive treatments [surgery, drugs or ECT] normally classed as medical.

Behavioural Therapy [Systematic De-sensitisation]

Behavioural therapy is based on Pavlov's theory of behavioural modification or systematic de-sensitisation. Behaviourists believe it unnecessary for people to have insight into problems in order to affect change, but merely to alter their behavioural patterns – i.e. the ruts we get into from time to time; reacting in certain ways to certain situations.

Systematic de-sensitisation is used where an unwanted habit has been formed, such as a phobia. The patient is gradually introduced to a programme of cutting down or introducing more [as appropriate] of the condition until they are literally re-programmed to behave in a different way.

Example 1
Smokers will be directed to cut down on cigarettes. They may be played videos of cancer-ridden patients or given hypnotic suggestions of how clean their lungs will be after giving up.

Example 2
An agoraphobic patient will be asked to gradually increase the distance they are able to walk from their home.

Most therapists find this type of therapy too reductive which is why cognitive behavioural therapy [recognition or insight] is more widely practiced. We are after all not dogs but thinking beings.

Behaviour therapy can be coupled with drugs or medications to prevent unwanted behaviours. It is best used as an adjunct to a form of talking therapy or psychotherapy.

Uses of Behaviour Therapy

- agoraphobia or other phobias
- anti-smoking therapy
- therapies connected with habits
  i.e. smoking, drinking, nail biting, drugs to prevent sexual perversions

Cognitive Behavioural Therapy [CBT]

Cognitive Behavioural Therapy is based on the model of connections between thoughts, feelings and behaviour. How we think about something affects how we feel about it and that in turn affects behaviour or attitude towards it. This is not rocket science; it is based on learning theory.

To make it easier, I have added a little extra tag as follows: arising thought – follow on thought – feeling – behaviour. The initial or arising thought is spontaneous and cannot be changed, however the follow on thought can be changed.

- The **initial thought** arises spontaneously from the unconscious and is not under our control.
- The **follow on thought** depends on our conditioning i.e. what we believe to be true about a situation.
- How we **feel** [consider] a situation follows the conditioned thought
- How we **behave** [respond] depends on the feeling

Consider this example.

- **initial thought** – it is raining
- **follow on thought** – I wanted the sun to shine today
- **feeling –** frustration and discontent
- **behaviour** – go back to bed

Figure 13 Cognitive Triangle of Insight

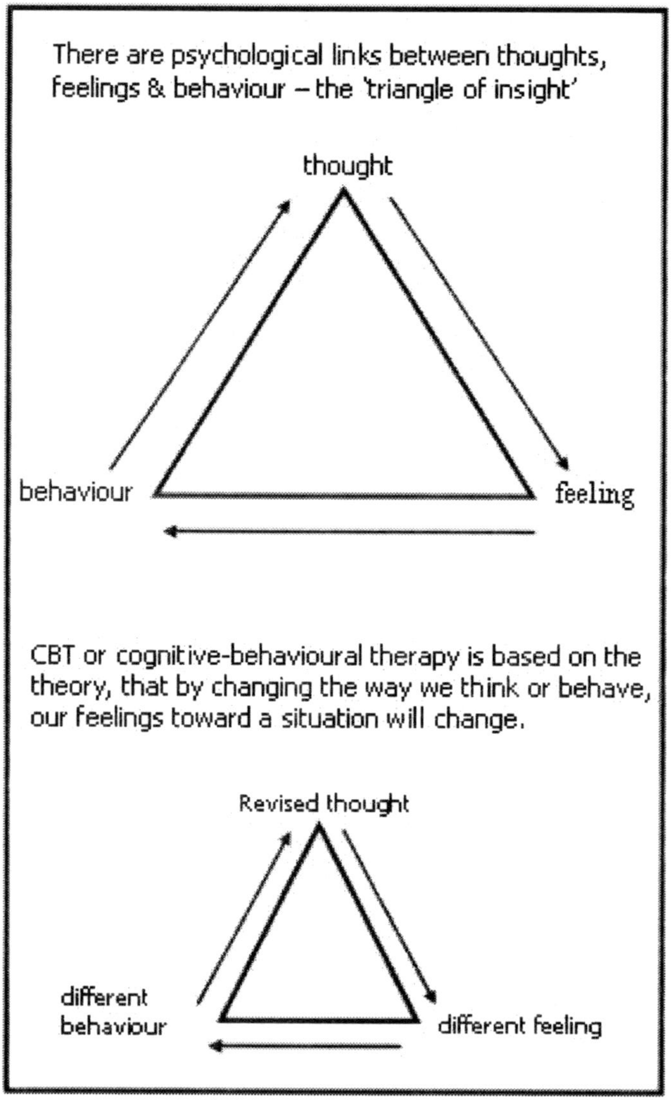

After modification, either through therapeutic input or our own altered thinking:

initial thought – it is raining
follow on thought – I wanted the sun to shine but at least the rain will water my garden
feeling – acceptance
behaviour – continue with the day's events

After a period of adaptation to the new thinking:
initial thought – it is raining
follow on thought – good, the rain will water my garden
feeling – contentment
behaviour – choose what to do that day

So, you can see that by modifying a thought about a situation [not the initial thought] you can actually alter the way you feel and behave. CBT therapists will say that you can also change the effect by altering your behaviour i.e. act 'as if' the rain is a good thing and it will similarly alter your feelings [attitude] towards the event or situation.

CBT therapists ask patients to record their thoughts feelings and behaviours and their altered responses. The therapy is useful with those who are able to gain insight into their problems but can be used to train others in behavioural modification way [i.e. as Pavlov taught his dogs].

Uses of CBT

- treating phobias
- depression of all degrees
- emotional problems
- behavioural problems

Key Learning 44 The Triangle of Insight
CBT is about learning to recognise thinking and behaviour patterns; the way you feel about the situation will change correspondingly when these two are modified.

Counselling, Psychotherapy & Psychology

There are many different schools of thought for counselling and psychotherapy and many overlaps which are not even clear to some professionals. This is why I think, for the short space I have here, to describe a few of the main types and to lump counselling with psychotherapy.

Umbrella Organisations

The two main counselling umbrella organisations each have members of from both disciplines:

- British Association for Counselling [BAC]
- United Kingdom Conference for Psychotherapy [UKCP]

Umbrellas are curious entities. I don't know if they exist in other fields but they appear to have developed a life of their own, overseeing the individual schools which make up their membership.

On the good side, they offer regulation but on the negative side, they are elitist. Those schools who cannot afford the umbrella organisation fees will eventually be squeezed out of existence as the Government tightens the noose on regulation, thus limiting training to those with large pockets. The schools did manage to self-regulate before these bodies came into power.

This is another reason the poor punter at the end of the line, the patient with no independent means, finds it difficult to find affordable treatment, whilst there are plenty of therapists around. Everyone is tied up in financial concerns. It is nothing less than a national disgrace and needs a return to the values these people claim to support.

Talking Cures

Talking cure is a term coined by one of Freud's patients, Anna O., to describe how Freud cured her during hypnosis. The term is now in common usage to describe all therapies which use talking rather than invasive medical techniques [drugs, surgery, ECT etc]. I sometimes explain to patients we cannot move a mountain;

however, if we consider the mountain to be made of individual rocks then over time we can move it. This is an analogy for how talking cures work. the patient gradually comes to recognise their faulty thinking or behavioural patterns or that there are better ways of living, or how relating differently to people can reap benefits.

Modelling

Medicine seeks to target a specific area, be it brain chemistry, neurons, or a physical system [heart, muscles]. Doctors can pinpoint neurons and systems by using brain scans, x-rays and diagrams of the human systems which have been scientifically drawn from life through examination of corpses. Early doctor-scientists drew heavily on this method before the invention of CAT scans and the like.

However, in dealing with the mind, it is more difficult to target a specific problem area. Although the brain is a physical organ, the mind is not. It is ephemeral. Existential problems are complex and cannot be drawn in the way that anatomists can draw the circulatory or the muscular system. Each mind is individual, the product of its human creator whereas we all possess the same physical systems.

So, therapists had to find another way of explaining the workings of the mind. What they came up with was modelling; diagrams which explained their theories in symbolic form. The diagram of the CBT triangle in this book is such a model.

Key Learning 45 Modelling

Modelling is making theoretical models for psychological concepts, enabling us to learn in symbolic form how the mind works.

Schools of Thought

So how did the schools separate? Many people think it started with Jung and Freud but in fact hypnosis is the oldest therapy and has been used from very early times.

Freud was a follower of Charcot and Breuer, the two men who modernised the use of hypnosis as therapy. Freud and later his disciple Jung spent their lives exploring the psyche and it is these two branches which spawned the whole line of psychotherapies [mind therapies] which include all the schools of psychology and counselling.

What happened thereafter, is that a pupil of a great theorist might develop their own line of thinking, based on what they had learned but maturing as their thinking developed. This theory might attract new followers [pupils or students] and thus a new school starts.

It is interesting exercise to trace back the various schools to their origins. I know this has been done in various books and websites but if you trace back the school of thought for your own school, you will get a greater sense of achievement and understanding of the theories.

So, your patient is both inundated with choice over the model they prefer but at the same time stymied by the cost of the therapy which is probably [for most working people] about **eight times** [minimum] **the hourly rate they earn** [based on minimum wage which is what a large chunk of the population is expected to live on]. That is what we call progress.

Let's take a look of some of the broader branches of theory, or schools of thought. I'm afraid I risk the accusation of reductionism, because it is impossible to reduce a school of thought to less than half a page; but there we are. I have interpreted what I have read of the following schools to the best of my ability.

I left out psychosynthesis, because there was such a negative reaction from the person I approached. If any school feels misunderstood they are welcome to write to me and put their viewpoint not make demands for non-publication. A pity as I had been interested in this school for some time.

I would like to relay this brief anecdote. The best teacher I had at University when faced with puzzled looks from a student did not say 'don't you understand what I mean?' but 'perhaps I need to explain that in another way'.

Theoretical Stances

Lest I be accused of favouritism [perish the thought!] I will place these in alphabetical order:

- analytical psychology
- gestalt
- Rogerian or Client-Centred therapy
- hypno-psychotherapy *
- psycho-dynamic
- psychology [behavioural therapy and CBT]
- Reichian [physical therapy]
- solution focused or brief therapy *

* these are linked but have many schools of their own

I will give a brief description of each. If you want to know how they work in more detail, I described some of them within the case histories in my book, **Understanding Mental Illness**.

Analytical Psychology

Jung coined the term personality as a model for the almost impossible to explain amorphous mass of ideas, morals, values, beliefs, ancestral symbols [collective unconscious] etc. which make up our self or personality.

If you think about it, this was an incredible undertaking and could not have been achieved in such a dynamic way without Jung's studies on world religion, spirituality, mythology and study of the psyche [mind]. The personality defines who we are and how we live.

Analytical psychologists look in a broader sense than probing individual problems. The aim is integration of the personality [the self] with its sub personalities [archetypes]. This process is lifelong and which peaks around mid life when the focus changes from outward doing [getting and spending] to inward thinking [reflection]. Jungian Analysts call this process individuation.

Working towards individuation, life's problems will be understood and integrated into the individual's experience. Problems are seen as part of the journey rather than distinct ends in themselves. Through this process of maturation and insight, the individual learns to recognise and avoid pitfalls.

In order to understand elements of the personality there are ways into the unconscious mind:

- through symbols expressed in dreams
- ancestral memories during reverie, moments of de ja vue

Jung's theories were never put together in a whole theoretical framework although he wrote many books on its individual elements. He felt his books spoke for themselves.

Key Learning 46 Jung & The Personality
Jung's life work was understanding the personality. It is the work of the therapist to lead the patient towards individuation.

Gestalt

"Life is not a problem to be solved but a reality to be experienced."
Kierkegaard

Gestalt follows the school of Fritz Perls, himself a student of psychoanalysis. It is an amalgam of psychoanalytic and humanistic principles, seeking to discover the whole person and their relationship to the world they live in, as experienced **in the now**.

If you read the epigram above by Kierkegaard, it neatly summarises the Gestalt view. Problems are not separate entities but are part of life experience.

Gestalt means unified or whole or the essence of something; it implies a complexity that cannot be reduced without taking something from it. In Gestalt, the environment is as important as the experiences of the patient.

Gestalt therapy is concerned with helping the patient into full awareness by all possible methods. Therapy is usually conducted in groups with group members acting as co-therapists. Thoughts, feelings, images from the past are brought into the present by asking the patient what they are experiencing in the here-and-now and exploring these issues.

Encounter Groups

Certain groups misappropriated this methodology. So-called encounter groups encouraged patients to relive past negative experiences whilst other members of the group supposedly made comments designed to change the patient's experience of the past event.

A friend of mine [now deceased] was encouraged to talk about her friend who had committed suicide by jumping from a building. She was already distressed, but one of the group started chanting 'tomato sauce' a chant taken up by several others. She told me that she could not wait for her turn, so that she could get revenge. Normally she was not to be that kind of person. This kind of behaviour clearly breeds bullying and not new perceptions.

Key Learning 47 Gestalt - the whole

It is difficult to summarise Gestalt, but this epigram will have to suffice 'the whole is more than the sum of parts'.

Rogerian or Client-Centred Therapy

Rogerian therapy is a humanistic style based on acceptance of whatever the patient brings, even if that might be shocking to the therapist. Carl Rogers was the most influential of the humanist group.

It is perhaps not surprising that Rogers major theoretical stance was unconditional positive regard of patients. He was religious, destined for the priesthood, when a chance visit to an overseas convention opened his mind to new ideas, and he decided to take up psychology.

Rogers felt that all humans [and indeed animals and plants] contained the seeds of self-actualization. Mental illness was, to him, this process gone astray. The task of therapy was to bring the client [Rogers' less pejorative term for patient] back to wellness by accepting them as they were. He saw the need for the provision of love and stability to re-ignite the process of actualization.

He called his therapy client-centred but it is also known as Rogerian therapy. The three basic elements for the therapist are:

1. **Empathy** – sympathy with the patient at an emotional level, without entering their feelings
2. **Congruence** – being open and honest
3. **Respect** – showing consideration and understanding

Some therapists are of the opinion that all Rogerian therapy takes is mimicking the words of the client:

> **Client** 'I feel blue'
> **Therapist** 'You feel blue?'

This is not only insulting the client but hardly likely to gain the level of therapeutic empathy which Rogers envisaged. The more likely progression of the dialogue is:

> **Client** 'I feel blue'
> **Therapist** 'So life doesn't feel good at the moment?'

Rogers was not merely talking about clients self acceptance and living in the now, but a full embracing of all of life; what he called: 'launching oneself fully into the stream of life'.

This kind of living would bring its sorrows as well as joys and was not for the people afraid of the powerful negative emotions. Full immersion into life was, he considered, the only way the client could self actualize.

Rogers completed a great deal of humanitarian work outside his therapeutic life; using his methodology to bring together warring communities world wide.

Key Learning 48 Rogerian or Client-Centred Therapy
Rogers taught total acceptance of the client, whatever they might bring to therapy. This is humanistic therapy.

Hypno-Psychotherapy

Much derided at one stage for what outsiders saw as its apparent simplicity hypno-psychotherapy is now a widely respected therapy.

Hypnosis was an old form of therapy going back centuries. In the nineteenth century Breuer and Charcot treated patients for hysterical paralysis. The treatment became popular and many students were attracted to learning its principles, including Sigmund Freud.

The hypnotic state is a natural one and is a very deep form of relaxation in which the conscious mind is bypassed and appeals can be made direct to the unconscious mind.

Hypno-psychotherapy is not just hypnosis. Students learn about psychological principles and other mind models and incorporate the tool of hypnosis into their therapeutic tool kit.

Milton Erickson & Solutions Based Therapy

There are many schools within hypno-psychotherapy. I described the basic theory of Ericksonian therapy [Milton Erickson] during my resume of a history of mental illness. The solution focused and brief models, and indeed NLP, have all been developed from Ericksonian thinking.

Erickson encouraged his therapists to understand the patient, by really listening to the language they used and getting into their symbolic map of the world; how they experience their world. Without this understanding, he believed, the therapist could not help the patient.

Erickson believed everyone possesses the skills to resolve their life problems, but these skills become clouded through life events. It is the conscious mind which blocks self belief and trust in the process of therapy. Hypnosis bypasses the conscious mind allowing direct access to the unconscious.

Erickson also used tasks for his patients and these sometimes appear outlandish. This is because we are reading them outside their context. Many therapists mistakenly copy these directive instructions, rather than listening to the patient.

Erickson had gone through a great deal of suffering in his life and utilised his knowledge for therapeutic purposes, not to gain power over people or make fun of them as some do.

One of the best examples is Erickson's market gardener patient who is depressed and has given up. Erickson does not talk about depression but gradually sends the man into a semi-hypnotic state by talking at length about plants and growth and sunlight. He helps the man into a renewed interest in life and of the part he plays in it.

Empathy is built between Erickson and his patient through the symbolism of the garden. There is no need to talk about illness or depression directly. Therapy is accomplished by re-establishing the man's purpose in life and his joy in his work.

Key Learning 49   Solution & Brief Therapies
Solution focussed, brief therapies and hypno-psychotherapy are based on problem solving and educational methods rather than psychoanalysis.

Psychology

The pioneers of psychological thinking were Freud and Jung whose work I have already attempted to explain. Psychology is the study of man's behaviour. Psychologists carry out behavioural experiments on animals, such as Pavlov's work.

They draw heavily on modelling to explain their theories, for example the CBT model in this book. Some psychologists work in research and never come into clinical contact with patients.

For further information, read the section on cognitive behavioural therapy.

Key Learning 50 Psychology
Psychology is the study of behaviour. Psychologists use modelling to extract theories by studying unusual [pathological] behaviour.

Reichian Therapy

Wilhelm Reich was initially a follower of Freud and the psycho-analytic model. However, he felt that the effect of the psyche on the physical body [Freud's libido] had not been sufficiently explored and this became his focus.

Reich believed that problems in the psyche lead to physical armouring whereby muscles become tightened and locked. His therapy consisted of physical exercises aimed at releasing physical tension and thereby releasing psychic and sexual tensions at the same time.

Part of his experiments were based on a mysterious energy he called orgone which had two types – orgone [positive and energy producing] and DOR or deadly orgone radiation. He developed an orgone accumulator, which was a shielded box people could sit in. Reich claimed this would cure patients of mental illness and relieve them of sexual and physical tensions.

Reich's radical beliefs brought him into conflict with the authorities and he was imprisoned for breaking an injunction which had been imposed on his selling of his accumulators. His books were burned by the authorities. Sadly, he died in prison of a heart attack before the value of his work could be recognised, as it has been in such practices as sexual therapy.

Key Learning 51 Reichian Therapy
A combination of thinking which links blocked libido [orgone] to muscular armouring in the body.

Family Work

Mental health workers now routinely work with the families of people with schizophrenia, to try to prevent some of the trauma and disruptions to family life. This is an adjunct to work with the patient.

Many families find it hard to cope with their relative's mood changes and tendency to withdraw from society, which can be misinterpreted as rejection.

Patients do not always recognise when they are ill and refuse medication so they become ill more often than they should. Lack of drug compliance can lead to family breakdown as the patient's symptoms manifest. This is distressful for everyone.

Family workers encourage regular taking of medication and help the patient prepare a care plan. This is a kind of advance directive made when the patient is well, with directions for how they want to be treated when ill.

Care plans can be comprehensive and creative. The plan includes a patient's list of their signs of oncoming illness, what they find helpful and how they do not want to be treated (the latter being just as important). Patients are encouraged to live a healthy and productive lifestyle which takes into account their illness.

There are many more therapies, stretching into the hundreds which I may explore in a future book, however for now let's move on to look at some of the alternative or complementary therapies, which generally fall outside the NHS remit.

Key Learning 52 Family Work

Family work is based on seeking measures to combat repeat episodes of enduring mental illnesses such as schizophrenia, but using a whole family rather than individual patient approach.

****

Summary of Key Learning Points:

Key Learning 44 The Triangle of Insight

CBT is about learning to recognise thinking and behaviour patterns; the way you feel about the situation will change correspondingly when these two are modified.

Key Learning 45 Modelling
Modelling is making theoretical models for psychological concepts, enabling us to learn in symbolic form how the mind works.

Key Learning 46 Jung & The Personality
Jung's life work was the study of the personality. A Jungian Analyst's work is in helping the patient towards individuation and wholeness; the maturation of the personality.

Key Learning 47 Gestalt - the whole
'The whole is more than the sum of parts'.

Key Learning 48 Rogerian or Client-Centred Therapy
Client-centred is a humanistic therapy. Rogers said that patients must be totally accepted, whatever they might bring to therapy.

Key Learning 49 Solution & Brief Therapies
Solution focussed, brief therapies and hypno-psychotherapy are based on problem solving and educational methods, rather than psychoanalysis.

Key Learning 50 Psychology
Psychology is the study of behaviour. Psychologists use modelling to extract theories by studying unusual [pathological] behaviour.

Key Learning 51 Reichian Therapy
A combination of thinking which links blocked libido [orgone] to muscular armouring in the body.

Key Learning 52 Family Work
Family work is based on seeking measures to combat repeat episodes of enduring mental illnesses such as schizophrenia, but using a whole family rather than individual patient approach.

'unless you undertake to try to do something beyond what you have already mastered, you will never grow' Ronald Osbourne

11 Alternative & Complementaries

Contents of this Chapter:

Arts therapies

The Arts therapies are becoming broader ranging and encompass a range of traditional arts;

- art
- music
- drama
- writing and bibliotherapy

The difference between these disciplines expressed as pure art and their use in therapy is interpretation.

An art therapist will help the patient interpret what they have drawn; in drama therapy, they will be encouraged to act out archetypal scenes from their life, perhaps with alternative endings being explored.

There is as yet no degree in writing therapy but I am sure that will come in the not too distant future. Many people have traditionally written diaries, stories, or kept scrapbooks of their lives as a means of reminding themselves of better times or recording their feelings.

Training in art therapies is limited to those who have degrees in their subject. There are, I am sure, many people out there in the community who would make excellent therapists who do not have such qualifications. However, this is the way the world is going.

Key Learning 53 Arts Therapies
Art practiced as therapy involves interpretation of the patient's work, which ever art medium is used.

Green & Eco Therapies

Green therapies are those which are not based on medical principles, and are connected with the environment. These are growing in popularity as traditional medicine wanes because of the public losing confidence in drugs as a cure for their existential problems.

Some enlightened authorities are looking into possibilities such as prescriptions for pets or library books but this is a rarity rather than the norm. There is little evidence base for the effectiveness of such therapies, but plenty of anecdotal or common sense for their use.

Reading, pets, walking, climbing and all sorts of outdoor pursuits, including therapeutic volunteering [for example, working with the National Trust on community projects] have long been used as forms of relaxation and for their therapeutic benefit. I covered some of these in more detail in 'Understanding Mental Illness'.

It is clear, as society seeks for respite from stress, for happiness and a new way of life, that beneficial exercise or hobbies will become more prominent in our lives – if we can somehow find the time to accommodate them!

Perhaps one day, like the duvet days in the USA, we will be allowed time off for relaxation. I am sure this will be beneficial all round.

Key Learning 54 Eco & Green Therapies
These are growing in popularity though rarely funded in the NHS. They include pet therapy, walking, green gym, therapeutic volunteering, bibliotherapy.

Spiritual Therapies – Mindfulness & Meditation

Spiritual therapies and pursuits are becoming more popular, even in mainstream medicine. 21st century jaded business people and those who work hard in bringing up families are seeking something missing from their lives; a gap left by the lack of religious life if we use the model of the mind-body-spirit balance.

Mindfulness is a simple type of meditation long used by Buddhists whilst doing daily chores – a simple awareness of concentrating on the task in hand. It sounds simple, but is difficult for those not used to doing one thing at a time or being able to relax.

Mindfulness is taught in some mental health departments not only for the benefit of patients but also hard-pressed practitioners. Again, there are many therapies of this type, which take into account the trinity of mind, body, spirit.

Key Learning 55 Spiritual Therapies

These have long been used in the East but in Western society are relatively new concepts. Mindfulness meditation is growing in popularity in the NHS.

Chinese Herbal Medicine

This is a surprising addition to the NHS pantheon, but nevertheless it has been proved effective in a whole range of situations, from physical to mental illnesses. There are now many Western practitioners as well as those Chinese doctors who have imported their skills and long training to the West.

The Chinese have been using natural remedies for centuries. Chinese Herbal Doctors train for many years. They use all the parts of a plant – root, bark, stem, leaves, flowers, buds as well as minerals. The resulting medicines often look strange, smell odd and taste awful but reputedly are very effective.

Chinese practitioners use a combination of methods including acupuncture, dietary therapy, tai chi or qi gong. Tai Chi is a soft marshal art and qi gong a form of slow but methodical exercise.

The University of Bristol Botanic Garden set up a Chinese herbal garden in 2000 as a joint project with the Register of

Chinese Herbal Medicine and this will be used in both teaching and future research.

Key Learning 56 Chinese Herbal
Chinese Herbal Medicine is based on holistic principles of unity of mind, body and spirit. As well as plant remedies, practitioners use exercise, diet, acupuncture, Tai Chi.

Healing

Healing is the most ancient and culturally widespread of therapies – the laying on of hands in order to affect healing of mind and spirit. A popular version is Reiki.

There is much anecdotal evidence for the effectiveness of this practice and some scientific evidence. The benefits of a good therapeutic relationship between therapist and patient has long been known, as has the simple matter of human contact.

Whilst both religious and secular organisations offer courses on healing, there have been natural healers in existence for thousands of years. It will be a shame if this simple folk remedy is over-regulated which will make it hard for ordinary people to access.

Humour Therapy; Gesundheit Institute

I could not leave this section without mentioning a controversial therapy which is nevertheless popular among its patients and professional staff.

You may have seen the movie Patch Adams; if not, do try to get a copy of it. The movie is the fictionalised version of how Dr Patch Adams came to set up the Gesundheit Institute, which he is currently trying to fund in the US.

Dr Adams is a different kind of Doctor who believes in a humane kind of health care based on mutuality of interest and shared values. He is also a professional clown, using humour to bring his patients back to wellness. His team of fellow clown-doctors have been visiting hospitals and clinics world wide to spread their brand of human kindness therapy.

Dr Adams hopes for a free hospital has been kept alive for over 30 years; a healing place where professionals and patients live-in on an equal footing. It is sad he has not yet secured the funding he needs for the main building, although they have now purchased the land and have the plans.

Humour is very much on the menu of treatment and as far as possible medication is not used. Mentally ill patients are treated and accepted as they are, even with bizarre symptoms. The few who cannot be treated by the Institute are referred elsewhere. The treatment is not one way but largely an equal healing relationship between professional and patient.

Dr Adams hopes patients who come to stay in the hospital will offer their professional skills to other patients who need them – he cites the example of a mechanic possibly offering to repair cars for those who cannot afford this. This kind of social capital [mutual benefit system] goes beyond mere medicine into a vision of a new social system.

Dr Adams' vision is way outside conventional thinking about healthcare but is exactly what his patients ordered. Let me finish with a quotation from Dr Adams:

> Good health [is] deeply related to close friendships, meaningful work, a lived spirituality of any kind, an opportunity for loving service and an engaging relationship to nature, the arts, wonder, curiosity, passion and hope. All of these are time-consuming, impractical needs. When we don't meet these needs, the business of high-tech medicine diagnoses mental illness and treats with pills.

Comic Relief take note – this is a relevant cause and could do with support outside the US; perhaps the first model could be built in the UK? I wonder if my email to Lenny Henry has seeded any thoughts... Watch this space.

Key Learning 57 Humour Therapy; Social Capital
There are new ways of thinking about healthcare systems afoot in the US, including mutuality and the use of social capital.

Choice of Therapy

I have often been asked about choices by patients who have no prior experience of being in any kind of therapy but are tired of being given medications and pills. They don't know who to go to for help and find the explanations offered by therapists confusing.

I think the best way of helping this choice dilemma is by analogy. This applies whether you are a patient, client or mental health worker advising someone.

If you go to a garden centre looking for a plant to fill a gap in your garden, you might find plants that you like the look of. So, you read the plant label and see if it will suit the soil in your garden, if it likes sun or shade, dry or wet conditions – in other words, if it will **suit the conditions** which you are going to apply to it.

It must also be suitable for the plants you have there already – in other words, it must **fit the environment** the existing plants are fixed into [no use trying to fit a knot garden in the middle of a cricket pitch].

You may also have a budget; if it is tight you are going to hesitate before buying one expensive tree fern – so, it must **suit your pocket**.

If you don't like the look, colour or smell of the plant, what is the point of buying it; so, you **go on your instincts** about what is most suitable.

Therapy is serious business – it can hurt your pocket more than cure your mind. You might select the wrong therapist a few times but don't stick with them if it's not working.

Key Learning 58 When Considering Therapy

Take into consideration; instinct, pocket, evidence, conditions and suitability of purpose.

****

Summary of Key Learning Points:

Key Learning 53 Arts Therapies
Art practiced as therapy involves interpretation of the patient's work, whichever art medium is used.

Key Learning 54 Eco & Green Therapies
These are growing in popularity though rarely funded in the NHS. They include pet therapy, walking, green gym, therapeutic volunteering.

Key Learning 55 Spiritual Therapies
These have long been used in the East but in Western society are relatively new concepts. Mindfulness meditation is growing in popularity in the NHS.

Key Learning 56 Chinese Herbal
Chinese Herbal Medicine is based on holistic principles of unity of mind, body and spirit. As well as plant remedies, practitioners use exercise, diet, acupuncture, Tai Chi.

Key Learning 57 Humour Therapy; Social Capital
There are new ways of thinking about healthcare systems afoot in the US, including mutuality and the use of social capital.

Key Learning 58 When Considering a Therapy
Take into consideration; instinct, pocket, evidence, conditions and suitability of purpose.

'Even the smallest person can change the course of the future'
J R R Tolkien; 'Gandalf', Lord of the Rings

12 Aftercare

Contents of this Chapter:

Dealing with Facts: There is No Cure

There is no cure for mental illness, because there is no cure for life itself. We all must regard ourselves in remission, whether suffering schizophrenia or stress. I believe there are several positive things about this way of thinking:

1. awareness of a condition leads to better self care
2. monitoring your own mental health is a preventative
3. the more we can learn, the more we maintain control

There is a certain equality in realizing that everyone will have to deal with stress whether or not that leads to major mental illness. Everyone will have to deal with bereavement or loss, which are known factors in depression.

No one is the perfect human animal. Somewhere in your patient's system, in fact all of our systems, is an Achilles heel whether that be a physical, spiritual or mental disorder.

The prevalence of depression is 1:4 and that of schizophrenia 1:25. There are many people with undiagnosed personality disorders. People who believe themselves perfect are most likely to have a problem whereas awareness, without fear, of mental problems is most likely to bring the required help. The word normal is really a measuring point and has no meaning.

Key Learning 59 No Cure
The sad fact is, there is no cure for mental illness. However, awareness of a condition is likely to more help.

Support for Chronic Mental Illness

There is very little at present in the way of aftercare, except for known patients with long standing mental illness. For such patients there are excellent services provided by mental health charities that provide ceaseless and tireless work on behalf of their clientele.

In the NHS, that crumbling bastion of an antiquated system, there are the Community Mental Health Teams, comprising a mixed range of professionals:

- Psychiatrists
- Mental nurses
- Psychologists
- Social workers
- Occupational Therapists

Currently, they treat both patients and some referrals from Primary Care. I described these teams more fully in **Understanding Mental Illness**.

Rivalries were always rife in these teams. Hopefully, when [and if] the new mental health worker grades start to filter through the system, so that everyone has an equal training at the beginning of their career, the sense of superiority will start to melt away. I hope so.

Assertive Outreach Teams and teams set up to deal with early intervention methods for psychosis also offer support to chronically ill patients who are known to have regular relapse patterns.

Within communities, there are **Rehabilitation Units**, where patients who need some support but will eventually be able to fend for themselves can live for a short time before being re-settled within the community.

And of course, there are the few remaining patients from the asylum days who continue to live in the **group homes** set up in the 1990's. These were pioneers of community living with all the anxieties and difficulties that entailed. They were really the end of an era for the treatment of mental illness.

Key Learning 60 NHS Aftercare
Resources are severely lacking in the NHS, but good clinical staff do what they can despite the limitations.

Support for Day Patients

In the last few years Primary Care GP's have increasingly been offering counselling in their surgeries and some have also taken on mental health professionals who were formerly part of a CMHT [Community Mental Health Team].

At your GP surgery, you might ask to be referred for counselling but be offered no more than a set of four to six sessions. There is no choice over therapist in Primary Care.

Although brief therapy is useful for short term life or emotional problems, it does not resolve problems which need supportive counselling or psychotherapy; for example abuse, bullying, severe emotional problems, bereavement or long term depressive illness.

Key Learning 61 Brief Therapy - Not a Panacea
Although brief therapy is popular in the NHS at the present time, it is not a panacea. However, no therapy can claim to treat every condition; suspect those which do.

Self Help

There is one avenue of support which has been growing, and that is information on the Internet. Our American cousins are very organised in that respect and you can find a great deal of useful information for patients, free of charge.

However, do watch what you recommend to patients. Stick to mental health charities and universities, pukka news sites like the BBC or professional ones like the Royal College of Psychiatrists who provide free information leaflets for home printing.

Counselling Charitable Organisations

Many counselling charitable organisations started off with good intention, to provide trainees with training which was paid for by charitable donations [trainees were still expected to provide a donation and to give free services on completion of training for a fixed period].

Their trainees now charge NHS patients at private fee rates, using NHS rooms in Primary Care, often for free. They say these rates pay for the service but they also cover the cost of administration, offices etc. They have become businesses.

Their 'reduced rates' [around £20 per hour for the impoverished] are steep, considering most impoverished people are on national minimum wages of just over £5 an hour.

I don't know if the charities that gave this money are aware of this practice. This is one of the reasons why there is still, after all these years, a lack of affordable counselling services for those who really need them. They need to get their heads together to find a solution and fast.

Key Learning 62 Self Help

Self-help is a growing and popular means of treatment. It is often free by way of books, the Internet and libraries.

Therapeutic communities

As a sort of response to public anxiety about personality disordered mentally ill patients. I want to briefly cover therapeutic communities.

Therapeutic communities cater for those who do not have the social skills to live in the community, but can be trained to do so. They are mainly personality disordered patients, frequently imprisoned.

I mentioned one well known therapeutic community in HMP Grendon, which won an award for their work in this area.

There is not much research in the effectiveness of this treatment but that which has been carried out gives positive results. Patients and staff live together on an equal basis, with decisions shared by both. A great deal of self-disclosure is required and all patients are expected to join in therapy groups, individual analysis, work and social events.

The emphasis is on learning social skills and having unacceptable behaviours brought into the open so that the patient becomes aware of their maladaptive behaviour. The community can reject those who refuse to obey the rules.

This seems, in principle, to answer the needs of this group for a place in a society, modification of behaviour and a sense of belonging which this group of patients are unlikely to have experienced before [many will have been abused as children].

There are always outcries against these patients but little sense of understanding of why they are as they are. They are the outcasts of society. I am not asking they be loved and liked, because most people find this impossible, just that humanity can be shown to a group who had their lives taken away at an early age. As a so-called caring society – can we exclude people, whatever they are deemed to have done?

Positive Aspects:

- Man is a social animal - living in communities is the norm.

Overleaf-Therapeutic Communities

Figure 14 Therapeutic Communities

Patients and staff live together,
in the same environment.

Individuals are more self aware in a supportive group, where there is both mental and physical security

Negative Aspects:

- Groups can scapegoat individuals
- People develop different characteristics in groups to when they live alone – when they move outside the community, their behaviour might modify in a negative way
- Patients and therapists can become institutionalised

Key Learning 63 Therapeutic Communities
These provide care for those who are otherwise marginalised from the community; for example, patients and prisoners with severe personality disorders.

****

Summary of Key Learning Points:

Key Learning 59 No Cure
The sad fact is, there is no cure for mental illness. However, awareness of a condition is likely to more help.

Key Learning 60 NHS Aftercare
Resources are severely lacking in the NHS, but good clinical staff do what they can despite the

Key Learning 1 Brief Therapy - Not a Panacea
Although brief therapy is popular in the NHS at the present time, it is not a panacea. However, no therapy can claim to treat every condition; suspect those which do.

Key Learning 2 Self Help
Self-help is a growing and popular means of treatment. It is often free, by way of books, the Internet and libraries.

Key Learning 63 Therapeutic Communities
These provide care for those who are otherwise marginalised from the community; for example, patients and prisoners with severe personality disorders.

Dr Susan Parenti's paper – A New Vision for the US Health Service – could this be for us?

Sod's Law that permission arrived to quote the following just days after I sent in the final material for this book. This was unavoidable as I only found this entry very recently. However, as this material is very interesting I would like to quote it verbatim. Please pass this onto anyone, clinicians within or outside the NHS, whom you think would consider this material as a discussion point towards effecting change – because change is very necessary in the way our own NHS is being run.

Readers of my other books on mental illness will be familiar with my view, that the NHS is a crumbling ruin of what it might be, and despite sterling efforts by clinicians has been badly managed and financed for so long that it cannot survive in its current form. This view is by no means uncommon.

When I inform readers, that 1 in 7 clinicians are being bullied in the NHS, this comes as no surprise to many. Bullying is one of the features of organisations that are badly run, under-funded, not properly supervised or audited and with inadequate management in many areas; people without the skills or values to undertake this difficult work. If you find this hard to believe, there are many confirmatory articles and figures to be found on the Internet, so I am not going to defend my stance.

Long having believed that the way forward is 'small is beautiful', my vision for a new NHS was of small, satellite local groups, run by clinicians – and especially trained in leadership and values. I nearly shouted 'hurrah' when I saw Dr Parenti's article [purely by chance as I was searching for information on Dr Patch Adams] whose vision for the NHS in the USA could be a mirror image of a new vision for the UK NHS.

Dr Parenti believes that change IS possible, from clinicians who remain on the inside. I have resigned from the NHS, after disgraceful circumstances I am prevented from discussing, but will continue to do my best to fight for a better deal for those who remain and whose work I respect.

I like the idea mooted by Dr Parenti, of 'perturbation' – those ripples and slight movements which can cause great changes [for the better] to happen – without causing ill feeling or the violent opposition which does no one any good. David CAN win over Goliath; by strategy, fairness and determination.

As I have only recently been given permission to quote this article, please excuse my lack of commentary and also the fact that I have quoted the article as I found it. I hope none is missing, as the original has been taken off the site pending Dr Parenti's upgrading of the material.

I hope Dr Parenti will excuse my lack of preparation – but I felt it important that readers should see the source material, which will be available on the website of the Gesundheit Institute. The URL at the time this book was published:

http://patchadams.org/speakers/bio-susan_parenti.html

Quoted from Dr Susan Parenti's paper

[nb 'to be designed' denotes areas not fully explored as yet]

"The first position is the status quo: the health care system as developed by entrenched health system industries (hospital, insurance, pharmaceutical, information technologies—with government primarily acting as their watchdog). The medical profession of doctor—its history of professional sovereignty—now no longer provides the bottom line in health care. The bottom line belongs to a different bottom: Big Business.

We add a third position—whole system design—our frontline, can-do position: **Do it local, do it now, do it small, link with all.**

Given that there's a call for fundamental change in the US health care system, we respond by saying---that means, design something that DOESN'T act like a corporation.

PERTURBATION

Perturbation is the action of desperate and thoughtful people.

Perturbations are ideas/actions that put the system on the spot with the aim of destabilizing it, of making it trip on itself. When thinking of perturbations, we aim at the system's moving itself in a new direction under its own weight and inertia, as it attempts to compensate for our putting it on the spot. This is different from reforming or improving a system, where we aim at ourselves moving the system.

We turn to perturbation when we humbly admit that folks, we're in a David-and-Goliath position here as regards to change of health care system, in that:
1. the system we want to change is in the control of people/institutions who have power over us;
2. the system as is—unchanged—benefits them enormously;
3. these people/institutions have no intention of allowing change of that system, no matter how reasonable and ethical the arguments for change, no matter how compelling the evidence of human suffering and human waste, no matter how many compromises activists are willing to make towards these people/institutions.

In terms of perturbation, we do have a chance: the health care system in the US is so big, so complicated, so bureaucratic, with parts unable to connect to other parts, so insensitive to the mood of its environment, so unable to see its consequences—that falling by means of its own weight is a possibility.

Do we have a choice about anything in health care systems? Yes. Where we have a choice, there we can design.

1. Health care interactions inherit a culture of hierarchy, rank abuse, posing. This is something a group of people, in shaping their health care facility along the lines they want, can support, oppose, change, alter. —this is something that can be designed
2. In our consumerist culture, health/sickness is identified as being an individual property—a person sees her health as her own individual state, she battles against her disease, alone. (This, in the face of many studies that show a person has better health outcomes if she feels her wellbeing integrated within that of a larger group.) A group of healers/designers can come up with a language—frames and metaphors—that oppose this isolationist consumerist tendency, and situate the health of the individual with the health of a group. —this is something that can be designed
3. Health of the staff as important as the health of the patient — this is something that can be designed
4. **Participating in health as a people's popular movement** Commercial culture names a patient as consumer and a doctor/nurse as provider. Given this framing, health care interactions are experienced as a form of shopping, for both patients and healers. Beyond stopping at the counter to get a

pill, patients in the United States do not participate in health, health care, or health care systems. Designers can oppose this state of affairs and make elements in their facility (**by means of language, imagery, structure**) that enable popular participation in all aspects/levels of health, health care, and health care system. —this is something that can be designed

5. **Nesting** Currently health care has been nested in bureaucratic and financial institutions. This can be counter-acted: healing interactions need to be protected by nesting them in larger *beneficial* social groups. —this is something that can be designed
6. **Solidarity** We need to rescue the concept/feeling/action of solidarity from North America's garbage heap. In the current culture, each person feels "you're on your own", "everyone for himself". Thus under-staffing of nurses is experienced as the nurses' problem, not the problem of the doctor, medical student, patient, family, technician. This reveals a lack of solidarity between people whose interests are fundamentally in common. This reveals that the lines of solidarity need to be refreshed and redrawn. There need to be discussions about whose interests are being represented. Does the design move in the direction toward creating constructs in which solidarity between the greatest number of different people/groups is supported? —this is something that can be designed
7. **Decision-making** Who makes decisions? Is decision-making about health care system dilemmas communicated to/from the people? Does the health care system *listen*, in addition to *talk*? —this is something that can be designed
8. **Communication** How is information communicated and disseminated? Where is it? —to be designed
9. **Motivation of actors** Who stands to benefit? In whose interests are decisions made? Are the motivations of the others clear to each? Differences of power? —to be designed
10. Do people seek out health care, or does health care come to them? Is the health care system visible only when a sick person looks for it, or does a person have the sense she is nested in care? —to be designed
11. **Cure or care?** In the health care facility, is there a behavior which values cure over a commitment to care? —to be designed

12. **Spaces** Does the space (rooms, hallways, waiting rooms) support the values we want? —to be designed
13. **Presentation of self in everyday life** The way healers, staff, and patients act in everyday life is a choice and can be a tremendously valuable input to desirable health care interactions. There is no neutral interaction. —to be designed

The health care crisis is, amongst other things, a crisis of bankrupt ideas. People recognize that things need to change; they do not recognize that something has to be *made up*.

THE ANSWERS

Systems are circular; something which seems to be a cause turns out to be an effect of something else, and so on. Where to start?

If a system of **one payer, single tier, universal access** is created, then hopefully that will lead to a significant change in many other aspects of the culture of care in the system.

Designs where the **health care relation *shapes* the system, and where the system *protects* the relation**. If a group of health care providers at a clinic are involved in designing their practice, our hope is that a change in the culture of care will open the way to a change in the funding of it, or at least make people more susceptible to that change.

We say—local initiatives for the good of the public renew the sense of confidence in a group of people governing. **Campaign universally, design locally.**

Our strategy is this—rather than priding ourselves in working with organized business, we want to oppose and **expose the undesirability of market-controlled health care** and to **popularize a hands-off-health care**, corporations!! sentiment in Americans and in business-people themselves.

The abundance of bureaucracy in the medical system—the paperwork, the overseeing of diagnostic decisions by insurance companies, etc.—is not an error in the system. It is the *intended consequence* of the current system. **The system is being maintained at the expense of the well being of its members.**

Talking Points

1. We question at every opportunity the appropriateness of market capitalism to control (nest) the delivery of health care. We discuss the

limits of free markets and the need for non-market regulation of experiential goods (a term in economics for services whose outcome is uncertain). We point out that in the case of a relationship dominated good such as health care, cutting costs in overhead results in cutting care itself.

2. We debate the assumption that health care is (needs must be) expensive. The expense of health care is not a property of health care in itself; the expense is an engineered condition, a consequence of the present design. We debunk the framing that health care will always be costly by making reference to counter-examples.

We invite media and wireless activists to demonstrate how the use of technology in health care can be free.

Every time the question, "Who will pay for this expensive system" is asked, we balance this with our question, "Who has been profiting such that this system is expensive?"

Health care, by its nature, is inexpensive—it's primarily a relationship along with some tools. We keep that image in mind so that we avoid playing into the assumptions of the market. The "high cost of care", the "complexity of the system" are frames that fuel the symbolic capital of the current system.

3. We caution that when big business says "we're committed to cutting costs in health care" this DOES NOT mean "we're committed to making health care inexpensive". It doesn't mean that. Within market capitalism cutting costs means lowering overhead (workers' wages, resources) to keep profit at margins attractive to investment capital. It *does not* refer to lowering the cost of health care so that it's easily available to us who need it. Market forces always say they want to cut costs; the question of reducing their profit margins is never brought up.

4. We rename the health care system the 'disease management system'. When a person gets into the medical system, that person is getting disease management not health care. Disease management is a far smaller domain than the domain of health care. Health care is a huge domain of interactions, happening primarily outside the medical system, available to all, only not organized. John Glick, MD says, "Every moment is a health care moment". When does health care start? — when you decide to take a walk early in the morning? When you feel like you're getting a cold and a friend gives you echinacea drops in a cup of tea?

What is health care at its indispensible minimum? Against the noise tunnel of the expensive and complicated disease management system we need to keep in mind the simplicity of a desirable health care relation: it's a bi-directional relation of care, always available, always findable—as a matter of fact you don't have to look for it, it looks for you. One has a sense of being inside caring, of being nested in care—there's someone to turn to, to talk to, they suggest a few things to do, you do them, you turn to them again.

The protection of this simple relation, of its friendly permeating steadfast thoughtful presence, is the primary function of any system/culture built around it. Thus the system/culture would be so designed that this relation is either freely offered or offered at a low cost (supported by communal and social structures in a variety of ways); that the formation of any bureaucracy around it would be a sign of malfunctioning or predators, and steps would be taken to eliminate that; that creativity and variety would go into the design of the supporting nest into which the relation is put, and into the relation itself. So einfach.

5. Do we attempt to work with market institutions to change health care? Organized business is interested in discussing financing and administration, not health or health care. Thus, to sit down at the table with these major players in health care industries means to sit down with people who frame every discussion of health/health care as a discussion of money and administration. If any other consideration is brought up, they will look at you with a patronizing eye—after all, they know their business—and turn it back into a discussion of financing. So we *can* sit down with them at the table, but we have to realize we're sitting down with opponents to any direction of creating a desirable health care system available to all.

6. We need to garner support from business people, on a person-by-person basis, for hands-off-health-care initiatives. To appeal to faith communities whose morals lead them to ethical political positions. Every businessman has his fatherhood looking over his shoulder; has his son-hood, brother-hood. Every businesswoman is also a mother, daughter, sister, friend. Do they want to overhear, in the waiting room, that cutting costs was a factor in why their grandchild died on the operating table? At some point in their lives, someone they care about will be in the system too. Their own pricey insurance policies cannot be transferred to everyone they care about.

7. We consider what is happening to health care in the US a local version of the same market theories that initiated Structural Adjustment Programs across the globe by WTO and World Bank. (Structural adjustments' primary focus is to shape institutions/countries so that they're attractive to long distance investment capital.)

Structural adjustment policies have been tried in South America, and met, in an increasing number of cases, with resistance. Let's link our resistance to structural adjustment policies at home to the resistance made by allies across the globe who are also fighting these policies.

Final Remarks

The components of what we're calling 'Whole System Design' are two calls: one is a call for a variety of designs of those elements that will be become the culture of health care; and the second is a call for the sentiment: "hands off health care, big business" to become infectious in the Americas. Both these calls are efforts to perturb the current system.

In 2006, people in the United States have a diagnosis of the problem of our health care system that is clear and intelligent. If you read blogs/letters/emails from the common person they articulate their discontent with the health care system in a sophisticated way. (See membership polls conducted in spring, 2006, by MoveOn.Org). People want a fundamental change in the health care system. This means, we want a change in the fundamentals.

We need to be prepared for the language/framing in response to this desire for change. When Medicare Plan D came out in May 2006, it was a 122-page document with lots of complicated sections, written for older Americans, telling them how to get pharmaceutical drugs. 122 pages? Huh? How was this allowed? Did the writers lack schooling, lack funding, lack time to do a better job? We don't think so. Plan D was a linguistic display of 'passive intervention'.

We need to watch out. The existing players (entrenched industries, along with their current protectorate: the government) will respond to our clear desire for fundamental change with an engineered Tower of Babel. The column of language is coming at us now: fundamental change in the health care system is re-framed as the question "who will pay for this expensive system?" as a debate between various complicated payment schemes, as a mandate for consumer choice. 'Universal insurance' will be used, to confuse us into thinking this means 'single payer'. The language will befuddle us, discourage us.

The temptation will be to leave the discourse around health care to the experts. They seem to know what they're talking about, right? None of these experts will challenge the structural power of the entrenched industries, the huge salaries of the health care corporations CEO's, the fact that pharmaceutical corporations top the chart for profit returns, etc.

Will we permit 'passive intervention', again? The statistic is cited, over and over again, that in the richest country in the world, nearly 48 million Americans do not get health care.

We say that in the richest country in the world, 300 million Americans do not get health care. Yes, of these 300 million, many people do get into the disease management bureaucracy, as they have insurance. But what is happening inside the medical system is no longer care; the 567,000 licensed doctors are not permitted to doctor; the 2.4 million nurses are being thwarted at nursing. The culture of health care in America is being morphed into something else.

When hospitals and clinics are businesses, and doctors/nurses become business people, who will we then turn to for health care?

November, 2006" [Dr Susan Parenti]

Interesting food for thought and I would urge you to look in a few weeks at the website for the new update.

****

I hope these two books have raised some interesting areas for you to take your studies further, answered some questions and also helped you to find more. I have written an extensive glossary for you and some recommended reading. You will find more reading in my book, **Understanding Mental Illness,** now in its 3rd edition, updated to reflect changes in the field.

Above all, enjoy your learning. Do not be put off by so-called experts. The field has broad shoulders and diverse avenues. Who knows, you could have a sudden insight which changes how you give [or even receive] care and that is a wonderful thing. Respect your patients and they will respect what you offer and this way you will enjoy a long career doing a worthwhile job.

I hope you enjoyed my company for a while. Do join me in another book but for now I wish you every success as you continue your journey.

Figure 15 Sources of Self Help & Aftercare

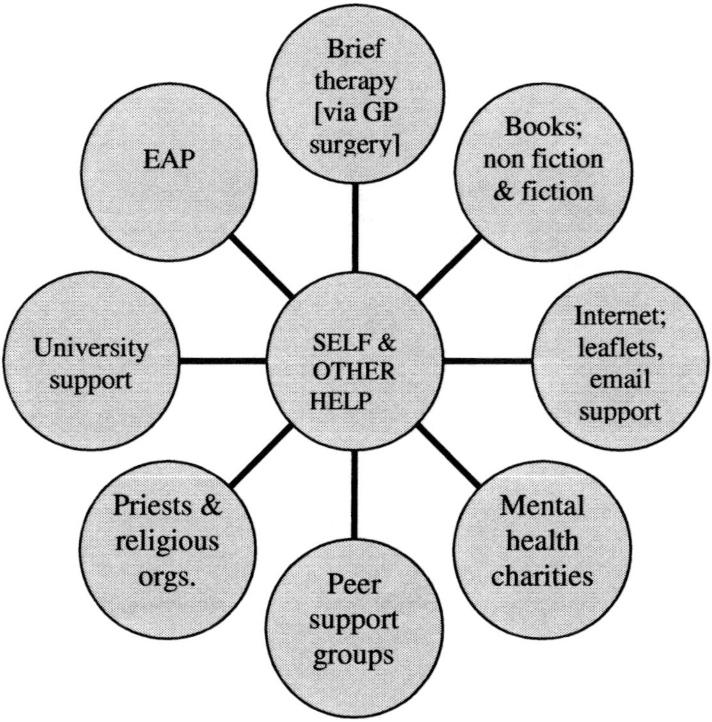

'If i knew that I would die tomorrow
I would plant another apple tree today'
MARTIN LUTHER KING

GLOSSARY

A

acupuncture	Chinese system of healing using needles to balance energies
actualization	self-improvement
acupuncture	Chinese medical treatment for re-balancing the body's energies
adenine	one of the four protein 'building blocks' of DNA
agoraphobia	fear of open spaces
alternative medicine	alternative to conventional medicine
altruistic	generosity of spirit
Analytical Psychology	psychological therapy [Carl Jung]
ancestor worship	culture of venerating dead ancestors
anhedonia	inability to experience happiness
anorexia nervosa	eating disorder; restricting food intake
antidepressant	drug reducing symptoms of depression
antimanic	drug reducing symptoms of mania
antipsychotic	drug - reduces psychosis
anxiety	state of arousal in which a person experiences unpleasant feelings
arachnophobia	fear of spiders
archetype	a specific character trait within the personality (Jungian theory)
armouring	process of the mind causing physical tensions in body [see Reich]
arts therapies	therapy for emotional problems using art, music or drama
Assertive Outreach	teams of mental health professionals working to prevent patient relapse
assessment	dorm of diagnosis, as used by non medical therapists
Asylum	Victorian institute for insane people. Literally 'a place of refuge'.
auto hypnosis	self hypnosis; a deep relaxation
avoidance	deliberately avoiding a situation because it is uncomfortable or fearful. Not pathological unless extreme.

B

BAC	British Association for Counselling (Umbrella organisation)
balanced personality	someone who has developed their mental and spiritual capacities
Bedlam [historic term]	mad uproar – originates from patient behaviour in Bethlam Asylum
behaviour	the things which we do; the way in which we react to situations
behaviour pattern	reacting in a consistent way to certain types of people/situation
behavioural therapy	a psychological therapy aimed at modifying behaviour (actions)
Bethlem or Bedlam Asylum	second oldest Hospital in England; a former Victorian Asylum
bi-polar	a mental illness; alternating episodes of depression and mania
bile (black bile)	one of the 4 'humours'; responsible for depression (see 'humour')
binge eating or binging	uncontrolled eating of vast amounts of food before purging it
blood/infection phobia	fear of blood, or of being infected by dirt, needles etc
BPS	British Psychological Society for training UK Psychologists
brain chemistry	the chemicals of the brain, produced by chemical transmitters
brain fever	historic term describing what is probably psychosis
brain scan	scans show electrical activity or physical damage in the brain
Breuer Joseph	famous Victorian practitioner of hypnosis; forerunner of Freud
brief psychotic disorder	mental illness of brief duration, brought on by stress reaction
Brief therapy	time limited therapies for existential problems [see Erickson]

British Association for Counselling [BAC]	umbrella organisation for counselling and some psychotherapy
Buddhism	spiritual order which follows the teaching of Gautama Buddha
bulimia	eating disorder, characterised by bouts of purging and vomiting

C

care plan	a written document, outlining proposed care for a client/ patient
carer	someone who cares for another person, usually voluntarily
case history	details of patient's life, with a psychological and physical history
case notes	records kept by therapists of client sessions, usually brief notes
Computerised Axial Tomography scan [CAT]	computer scan of whole human body; uses individual frames which are put together by computer
catatonia	mental state characterised by total lack of movement and energy
Catharsis or cathexis	Greek for purging; in psychology the 'letting go' of a negative trait
Charcot Jean Martin	famous Victorian Doctor and hypnotist; forerunner of Freud
'checking and testing'	trait of compulsive disorder; excessive checking
chemical imbalance	imbalance of mood-enhancing chemicals - serotonin or dopamine
chemical transmitter	the way brain chemicals are distributed to all of the brain cells
Chemist	scientist who has trained in preparing drugs and medications
Chinese herbal medicine	Treatment using herbs, also Tai Chi, acupuncture, exercise
Citizenship [curriculum]	New addition to national curriculum in schools – teaching ethics and standards for community living
claustrophobia	fear of confined spaces

client-centred therapy	Rogerian theory of unconditional regard for the patient
Clinical guidelines	sets of standards or rules used to carry out aspects of clinical work
Clinical Psychologist	psychologist who practices within medical setting
clinical responsibility	legal responsibility for patient's well-being
clinical trial	testing of new drugs
clinician	A person who practices medicine [clinic - Greek word for 'bed']
CMHT	Community Mental Health Team; mental health professionals
cognition	to recognise something
cognitive-behavioural therapy [CBT]	therapy for recognition and change of poor behaviour patterns
Collective unconscious	part of mind that retains ancestor or cultural myths [Jungian theory]
community	group of people living together for mutual support
complementary therapies	therapies not based on medical teaching; additional to medicine
compliance (of patient)	extent to which patients will willingly take prescribed drugs
compulsion	an urge to carry out a certain act or ritual
computer modelling	making accurate models of the body and brain using computers
conditioned response	theory that human behaviour depends upon an outside stimulus
conflict (mental)	two or more opposing events, motives, behaviours, impulses
conscious (mind)	part of the mind aware of its actions
contra-indication	one substance which affects another, as in chemicals in medicines
copyright	A law which forbids the copying of someone else's creative work
Coroner	officers who investigate unnatural deaths

counselling	one of the talking cures
Counsellor	mental health professional who offers a talking cure
Francis Crick	one of the 4 DNA pioneers see also Franklin R, Watson J, Wilkins M
crippled [historic term]	physically disabled. now considered a derogatory term
Crown Prosecution Service	the Government body which decides which criminal cases go to court [the police only provide the evidence]
crystal healing	healing by placing crystals on body; crystals supposedly give off therapeutic vibrations
cytosine	one of the four protein 'building blocks' of DNA

D

de ja vue	memory of reliving a past event
de-sensitising	therapeutic way of gradually exposing someone to their fear
delusion	ideas which are perceived as real, but are only in the imagination
dementia	usually irreversible brain damage with reduction in intellect
demon	another term for a devil or evil spirit
depot injection	monthly injection, usually in the buttocks or thigh
'depressive'	derogatory term for someone with depressive illness
depressive illness	mental illness, characterised by intense hopelessness and sadness
diagnosis	deducing illness from observation, or facts given by the patient
Diagnostic & Statistics IV [DSMIV]	manual for diagnosing mental illness as used by psychiatrists
Divine retribution [historic term]	punishment by a God or gods for mortals who broke divine laws
DNA	chemicals which carry the characteristics of human life

drug trial	Research of a drug's effectiveness before it is put on the market
drugs	medications; also used as a colloquial term for illegal drugs
DSM (IV)	see ' Diagnostic & Statistics Manual'

E

eating disorders	illness characterised by restricting food intake by various means
eco therapy	a 'green' therapy – green gym, walking etc
Electro Convulsive Therapy (ECT)	electric shock treatment given to treat chronic depression or the symptoms of schizophrenia
electric eels	historic treatment for madness; crude form of ECT
electro-encephalograph [EEG]	reading on a printed tape or monitor of electrical brain activity
empathy	an understanding of someone else's personal feelings
environment	setting in which we live
epigram	short quotation
epilepsy	interruption of electric flow to the brain causing fits
episodic [mental illness]	periods of mental illness followed by periods of normality
Erickson, Milton	pioneer of the brief therapies
ethical	responsibility to abide by the moral code in a particular situation
euphoria	extremely intense high mood
evidence-based medicine	medicine which is proven through research to be effective
evil spirits	imaginary entities who were blamed for episodes of madness
existential	the area of human existence
extrovert	outgoing, confident personality

F

forensic psychiatry	psychiatric work with criminal mental illness e.g. psychopathic

'fragmenting'	the experience of psychosis, or losing touch with the real world
Rosalind Franklin	one of the 4 DNA pioneers see also Crick F, Watson J, Wilkins M,
Frankl Viktor	Jewish psychiatrist; author of 'Man's Search for Meaning'.
free association	method devised by Freud for finding meaningful connections between specific words used by his patients
Freud Sigmund	founder of psycho analysis
G	
Galen	ancient Greek Doctor
General Practitioner	a medical doctor who practices in a general medical setting
genetic factor	attributed to inherited genes i.e. beyond control of patient
Gestalt	therapy concerned with unifying the person with their environment
Green therapy	see eco
Group Home	homes for several ex- patients living together
group therapy	a therapy conducted with one therapist and several patients
Guanine	one of the four protein 'building blocks' of DNA
H	
Hallucination, auditory	unreal voices or sounds
hallucination - visual	seeing things which are not real
Haloperidol	medication which prevents the symptoms of mania
healing	simple folk remedy with laying of hands on a sick patient
herbal medicine	chinese therapy using plant matter
hero	Jungian archetype - hero myth of birth, death & resurrection
'high'	exaggerated emotion
Hippocrates	Greek Philosopher and Doctor who made a study of the human mind

holistic therapy	Tri part Eastern belief encompassing mind body and spirit. All 3 must be in harmony to ensure mental and physical health
homeopathy	diluted herbs which mimic & heal the symptoms experienced
Humanistic therapy	therapy based on ethical thinking
humour or 'vital fluid'	in ancient medicine, 4 life-giving fluids in the body
Hypno-Psychotherapy	brief therapy using hypnosis
hypnosis	bypassing conscious mind by inducing relaxation
hypnotic state	state of relaxation [see trance]
hypothesis	initial assumption made in research; basis of scientific experiment
hysteria	historic term - loss of control
hysterical paralysis	paralysis due mental problem [see conversion disorder]

I

Idiot [historic term]	someone incapable of making decisions. Village idiot.
Imax	a huge screen which shows 3D movies
imbalance [brain]	brain's chemicals are not properly distributed; leading to illness
impulse	A powerful desire to do or act out
individuation	Jungian concept of the process of becoming a unique person
Inquisition	17th century church based court
insanity	state of mind where the mental processes are not functioning
insight	ability to understand the psychological situation
institutionalisation	deterioration of independence caused by long periods in hospital
Internet	a linked web of computers which can exchange information
introvert	thinking, inward looking personality

isolation	feeling different or separate from other people
J	
Jung Carl	founder of Analytical Psychology & modern psychotherapies
Jungian Analyst	follower of the Jungian school
L	
Laing R. D.	psychiatrist who believed mental illness was a social condition
Largactil	Early form of anti psychotic medicine
lay person	someone not formally trained in a particular discipline
Lazar or leper house	Institution for those with leprosy
legislation	laws passed by Government and approved by the Queen
leucotomy (lobotomy)	psychosurgery, cutting frontal lobes of the brain. Invented by psychiatrist Egas Moniz in 1935
libido	body energy, usually taken to mean sexual energy
librium	tranquilliser prescribed to many women - see also 'valium'
'life event'	an event which is vivid enough to be remembered long afterward
lithium	naturally occurring metallic salts used in the treatment of mania
lobotomy	see leucotomy
looney	insane; from early belief that the moon affected the mind. Term now considered derogatory
lunatic [historic term]	historic term for madness (belief that the moon caused madness)
M	
mad [historic term]	old term for mental illness now used derogatory or jocular way
madness	derogatory slang term describing people with mental illness

mania	mental illness, characterised by intense moods/ frantic behaviour
maniac	historic term - person with mania
manic	extreme excitement
manic episode	a period of mania
massage	manipulation of the muscles by outward pressure from hands
medical model	the theory of those who practice medicine i.e. use of medications
medication	drugs given to cure or alleviate the symptoms of an illness
meditation	peaceful contemplation of nature and the mind
melancholia	an early term for depressive illness
Mental Health Act 1983	Government guidelines for the treatment of mental illness
Mental Health Tribunal	group empowered to detain/ release psychiatric hospital patients
Mental Health Worker	similar to 'Rehabilitation Officer'
mental illness	illness of the mind, not 'physical illness; treatable not curable
Mental Nurse	therapist qualified to administer psychiatric drugs
mid life crisis	anxiety about achievements & the future said to occur at mid life
Milton Erickson	American psychiatrist who invented brief therapy
MIMS	manual of drugs and their characteristics, used by GPs
Mind	national mental health charity
mindfulness	the practice of a state of complete awareness in all tasks
model	a pattern or opinion used as an example; or a computer simulation
modelling (of humans)	Diagrams, theories or computer programmes which explain or replicate the functions of the human body or mind

mood	changing experiences of feelings e.g. happiness, sadness, anger
mood swings (rapid)	rapid mood changes
moral panic	short lived community concern, usually based on a news report
music therapy	type of art therapy using music to induce and counter mood

N

Natl. Health Service	Nye Bevan's system of public healthcare
Natl. Inst. of Clinical Excellence [NICE]	provides evidence based research for medical treatments
nervous breakdown	slang term for a mental illness; brief psychotic disorder
neuro transmitters (brain)	nerve cells containing chemical messengers affecting mood
NLP	'neuro-linguistic programming'; brief therapy method
noradrenaline	chemical transmitter in the brain (see also serotonin)
normal	there is no concrete meaning for this word but 'that which most people accept' is the nearest
normalizing	making a condition acceptable; can be positive or negative

O

obsession	preoccupation with something or someone, to the exclusion of all else
obsessive-compulsive disorder [OCD]	mental illness, characterised by obsessions and compulsions
Osteopathy	therapy involving manipulation of spine (see also chiropractic)

P

P [medication packs]	pharmacist must be present when this drug is dispensed
paedophile	man sexually attracted to children
panic attack	fear, usually onsets without warning
paranoia	extreme psychological fear
paranoid	form of schizophrenia with an

schizophrenia	obsession e.g. pursuit by devils
Parkinson's Disease [Parkinsonism]	disease characterised by tremors
Patch Adams, Dr	American psychiatrist who developed humour therapy
Pathology [pathological]	showing signs of some kind of illness
patient	term applied to people in a hospital or being seen by therapist
Pavlov, Ivan Petrovich	Neurologist who developed theory of conditioned response
peer	someone of the same level e.g. age group, intellect, interest
pen portrait or 'vignette'	- a written description, which describes a person
perception	A way of understanding something
Personality	part of mind that determines the personal qualities of self
pharmaceutical	relating to the pharmaceutical or drugs industry
pharmaceutical drugs	medications made of synthetic materials or plants in laboratories
Pharmacist	scientist - prescribes drugs
phobia	deep-rooted fear of something specific - e.g. spiders, flying, dirt
placebo	inert medication, given to some patients as part of drug trial tests
Plato	Greek Philosopher interested in the study of the mind
POM	prescription only drugs
Primary Care	G.P.s and the various therapists within G.P. Practices
Project Atlas (WHO)	WHO project; mapping mental health resources world wide
Prozac	SSRI drug for depression
psyche	human soul or mind; Psyche was a Greek goddess
psychiatric hospital	hospital for the care of mentally ill

Psychiatrist	a doctor with an extra qualification in psychiatric medicine
psychiatry	treatment and study of mental disorders
psycho	modern derogatory term for insane. Taken from Greek psyche = mind
psycho analysis	therapy developed by Sigmund Freud; analysing the mind
Psycho Analyst	therapist; practices psycho-analysis
psycho-dynamic	resolving current problems by understanding past relationships
psycho-educational	psychological training e.g. stress management, assertiveness
psychodrama	therapy involving 'acting out' scenes from the patient's life
psychological makeup	essence of someone's personality
psychology	the study of human behaviour
psychopath	personality disorder characterised by absence of conscience
psychosis	state of being out of touch with reality
psychosurgery	brain surgery
psychosynthesis	therapy based on integrating all aspects of the self
Psychotherapist	therapist using talking cure; enabling client to develop insights

R

reductive	when something is explained away without the full facts
refer	to introduce a patient
reflect	to consider something deeply
Rehabilitation Officer	therapist enabling mental health clients to live in the community
Rehabilitation Units	cross between a therapeutic community & psychiatric hospital
Reich, Wilhelm	founder of Reichian Therapy based on releasing psychic tension which has caused muscular tension
Reiki	method of healing by touch

religious	someone who devotes themselves to a particular set of beliefs
research	systematic study to add to the knowledge of illness and its cure
rite (or ritual)	ceremony to mark the main life changes e.g. birth, middle age
ritual (in illness)	repetition of a certain act which it is believed cures a situation
Rogers, Carl	founder of client-centred therapy
Royal College of Psychiatrists	UK professional body of Psychiatrists

S

St John's Wort	herb, said to be useful in treatment of depression
sanity	sound mind; able to distinguish between real & imagined events
scapegoat	sacrificed animal or person, who represents sins of community
'schizo'	derogatory term - someone with schizophrenia / mental illness
schizophrenia	mental illness with symptoms of delusions, hallucinations
School of Thought	a particular method of training; taught by an individual school
Social Care Institute for Excellence [SCIE]	provides evidence based research on social care [values based]
'section' / 'sectioning'	slang term meaning detained under the Mental Health Act
secular	lay members of the community
sedative	drug to calm nervous system
self hypnosis	voluntary state of deep relaxation - enables the unconscious mind
self understanding	process by which patients/clients learn about their characteristics
serendipity	an accidental discovery
serotonin	chemical transmitter in the brain (see also noradrenaline)
serial killer	someone who kills several people, using the same method

Shaman	priest, usually associated with North American Indian culture
shiatsu	Japanese massage using the fingertips on pressure points
'ship of fools'	16th century practice of sending lunatics to sea for a cure
Harold Shipman [MD]	a GP serial killer. Murdered up to 150 of his patients – convicted of 15
Skinner, Burrus Frederic	scientist - developed behavioural theory from Thorndike's theory
side effect	the unwanted effects of drugs (see also 'negative effect')
Situational phobia	fear of being in certain situations e.g. lifts, aeroplanes
Social Care Institute for Excellence [SCIE]	evidence based research for social care
social phobia	fear of social situations
solution-focused therapy	brief therapy; helps patients find solutions to life problems
Spanish Inquisition	medieval men delegated by the Pope to try and sentence witches
'speaking in tongues'	'babbling'-like speech; accepted in some sects as 'voices of God' and in others taken as a sign of illness
spiritual	accepting there is more than body and mind; morality & values
Spiritualists	religious sect who use Mediums to talk with the dead
SSRI's	specific Serotonin Re-Uptake Inhibitor; antidepressants
Standard[s]	set of instructions which provide the basis of the care or treatment
stigma or stigmatise	negative opinion fuelled by lack of knowledge. stigma = mark
Stimuli	what we perceive by hearing, seeing, touching, feeling
stress	the forces which determine action
sub personality	an individual characteristic of a person (see archetype)

subconscious	level through which material passes to the conscious mind
suicidal	clinical term; considering suicide
suicide	deliberately taking one's own life
Suicide Act 1961	act under which it is illegal to assist someone to commit suicide
Supervisor (therapy)	person a therapist sees to discuss and overview patients
supervision	learning through discussing patients with an experienced therapist
symbolic insight	as in dreams; we can learn about our true nature from symbols
symptom	A sign, usually of an illness
synthesised/ synthesis	combining individual chemicals for example to make new drugs
Thomas Szaz	Psychiatrist who believed mental illness was a social construct

T

Tai Chi	Chinese exercise and soft martial art
talking cure	therapies use talking to effect a cure
Temple of Light	ancient Roman place of cure for melancholia or depression
The Mental Health Act	in the UK, the Act concerned with care of the mentally ill
Therapeutic Community	a community of mentally ill residents and their therapists
Therapeutic relationship	healing relationship between therapist and their patient
Therapist	one who cures by using a therapy
therapy	cure for physical or mental illness; not necessarily medical
Thinking pattern	habitual way of thinking
Thorndike, Edward	behaviourist who worked on reward & behaviour responses
Thought disorder	as in schizophrenia; problems with normal linear thinking
thymine	one of the four protein 'building blocks' of DNA

trance — deep relaxation; the unconscious mind is open to suggestion

tranquilliser or 'tranny' — drug which suppresses or calms part of the nervous system

trepanning — cutting a small circle out of the skull; primitive psycho-surgery

U

unconditional positive regard — Rogerian therapy in which patient is fully accepted, warts and all

unconscious — part of the mind hidden from awareness

uncovered — term used in therapy to describe when something is realized

V

valium — addictive tranquilliser once widely prescribed to women

vignette — portrait or snapshot [used here to demonstrate certain symptoms]

virtual drug trial — testing new drugs using specialised computer programmes

virtual brain — computer model of a human brain

visualisation — imagining an event with the purpose of helping it become real

vital fluids — see 'humour'

voodoo — cult practised in Haiti connected with the raising of the dead for rites

W

Watson, James — one of the 4 DNA pioneers see also Crick F, Francis R, Wilkins M

Watson, John Broadus — Psychologist who developed the learned behavioural theory

White Paper — proposals from the Government for new pieces of legislation

Wilkins, Maurice — one of the 4 DNA pioneers see also Crick F, Francis R, Watson J

Witch — ancient term; a human servant of the devil, either male or female

Witchcraft — the practice of magic, for good or evil purposes

'word salad'	meaningless strings of words, manifested in schizophrenia
World Health Organisation (WHO)	a consortium of many countries who come together to improve standards in health care & carry out research into better health

Further reading

The following are in alphabetical order by subject.

THE ARTS ON LIFE

Paintings by **William Blake**
An artist who successfully portrays madness and suffering

The Plains of Heaven **John Martin**
One of a trilogy about The Day of Judgement

One Flew Over the Cuckoos Nest **movie**
Now made into an award-winning movie, the book is a fictional account about lobotomy. Although overstated it does give some idea of the tragedy of Asylums.

Shine **movie**
Based on the true story of concert pianist David Helfgott who had a nervous breakdown but later married and came back to the concert hall

A Beautiful Mind **movie**
Based on the true story of mathematician Dr John Nash, diagnosed with schizophrenia, he later became a Nobel prize winner

The Rain Man **movie**
Based on the true story of autistic savant Kim Peek

BIOGRAPHIES/DIARIES - mental illness

Kay Redfield Jamison **An Unquiet Mind**
Dr Jamison's own experience of manic-depressive illness

Jacki Lyden **Daughter of the Queen of Sheba**

Jacki's mother was diagnosed with mania and almost destroyed the lives of her family

RESEARCH & HISTORY OF MENTAL ILLNESS

Roy Porter **A Brief History of Madness**

An easy-to-read history of mental illness and its treatment.

American Psychiatric Association **DSM IV**

The diagnostic manual used by psychiatrists world wide to diagnose mental illness. See also websites

J Andrews, J Briggs et al **The History of Bethlem**

A history of the earliest of the Asylums.

Sainsbury Centre for Mental Health **Beyond the Water Towers**

Up to date expert papers on aspects of the treatment of mental illness, from asylums to the present day. Very readable.

CASE STUDIES & THERAPIES

Malcolm Macmillan **An Odd Kind of Fame: Stories of Phineas Gage**

The author is a well-known psychiatrist, This book is about the Victorian man who's accident inspired research into the functional areas of the brain, and also the infamous lobotomy.

Oliver Sacks **The Man Who Thought His Wife Was a Hat**

The author is a well-known psychiatrist who writes interesting vignettes about aphasia, an illness which prevents patients properly translating what they see.

Virginia Axline **Dibs, in Search of Self**
How a lost child was brought back into the world by a Psychotherapist.

Dr Kay Redfield Jamison **Touched with Fire**
A book covering the them of manic depression and creativity.

Carl Rogers **Client-Centred Therapy**
Carl Rogers famous book about his humanistic therapy.

Carl Rogers **On Becoming a Patient**

Interesting Websites

COMPLEMENTARY MEDICINE

http://www.baat.org/
British Art Therapy Association

http://www.acupuncture.org.uk
British Acupuncture Council

http://www.bcp.org.uk/
British Psychoanalytic Council

http://www.bsmt.org/
British Society for Music Therapy

http://www.bwy.org.uk/
British Wheel of Yoga

http://www.mctimoney-college.ac.uk/contact.htm
McTimoney Chiropractic

http://www.homeopathy-soh.org/
Society of Homeopaths

http://www.rchm.co.uk/
The Register of Chinese Herbal Medicine

MEDICATION

http://www.mentalhealth.org.uk/html/content/medication.cfm
Medication for mental health problems. An overview of the types available

http://www.rcpsych.ac.uk/info/factsheets/pfacanti.asp

Royal College of Psychiatrists factsheet on antidepressants

http://www.hospitalclown.com/
A different kind of medication – for those who dare to be different

MENTAL HEALTH ORGANISATIONS

http://www.who.int/mental_health/evidence/en/atlas_chapt_1_2_eng.pdf
The World Mental Health Atlas project [mapping global mental health services]

http://www.depressionalliance.org/
Mental health generally

http://www.samaritans.org.uk/know/statistics.shtm
Samaritans on-line

http://www5.who.int/mental_health/main.cfm?p=0000000149
World Health Organisation – mental health section

http://www.sane.org.uk/public_html/index.shtml
SANE & saneline (helpline) mental health charity website

http://www.together-uk.org/index.asp?id=1
Together mental health charity (formerly MACA)

http://www.rethink.org/
Rethink (formerly National Schizophrenia Fellowship) mental health charity

http://www.depressionalliance.org/
The Depression Alliance mental health charity

http://www.retreat-hospital.org/
The Retreat hospital. Care for anyone with mental health problems (York Retreat)

www.turning-point.co.uk
Turning Point, for mental health rehabilitation & counselling

www.mind.org.uk
MIND, the mental health charity

http://www.depressionalliance.org/
Depression alliance mental health charity

http://www.rcpsych.ac.uk/
Royal College of Psychiatrists - about mental illness

http://www.londonhealth.co.uk/carersnationalassociation.asp
Carers National Association

http://www.therapeuticcommunities.org/
Umbrella body for therapeutic communities

http://www.caringclownsinternational.org/
International clown medication

SCIENCE & TECHNOLOGY

http://www.bfi.org.uk/whatson/imax/about/imax-history.html
Imax cinema

http://www.ba-education.demon.co.uk/for/science/dnamain.html

DNA pioneers Rosalind Francis, James Watson, Francis Crick, Maurice Wilkins

TRAINING

http://www.rgu.ac.uk/subj/pharmacy/pharmacy.htm

School of Pharmacy web site

http://www.hull.ac.uk/home/prospectus/undergrad/social_work.html

Training in Social Work

http://www.npa.co.uk/

National Pharmacists Association

http://www.acpp.org.uk

Association for Child Psychology & Psychiatry

http://www.uncommon-knowledge.co.uk/milton_erickson/family_therapy.html

http://www.creativity.co.uk/creativity/guhen/erickson.htm

About the founder of all brief therapies - Dr Milton Erickson

http://www.newtherapist.com/20hitch.html

an amusing journey through brief therapy, in metaphorical style

http://www.n-shap-ericksonian.co.uk/Erickson.htm

Ericksonian brief therapy and NLP

Index

****